KNOWING KNOPPIX

A beginners guide to Linux that runs from CD

Disclaimer

KNOWING KNOPPIX

For Knoppix Version 3.3

Phil Jones

A beginner's guide to Linux that runs from CD

Intellin
Organization

www.intellin.org

Knowing Knoppix - A beginner's guide to Linux that runs from CD

Published by the

 Intellin
Organization

www.intellin.org

Disclaimer:

The software or related documentation in this book is NOT designed nor intended for use (whether free or sold) as on-line control equipment in hazardous environments requiring fail-safe performance, such as, but not limited to, in the operation of nuclear facilities, aircraft navigation or communication systems, air traffic control, direct life support machines or weapons systems in which the failure of the hardware or software could lead directly to death, personal injury, or severe physical or environmental damage ("high risk activities")

The author(s) and publisher(s) take no responsibility for damages or injuries of any kind that may arise from the use or misuse of the software or related documentation in this book.

The author(s) and publisher(s) specifically disclaim any express or implied warranty or fitness for high risk activities. The software and related documentation are without warranty of any kind. The author(s) and publisher(s) expressly disclaim all other warranties, express or implied, including, but not limited to, the implied warranties of merchantability and fitness for a particular purpose. Under no circumstances shall the author(s) and publisher(s) be liable for any incidental, special or consequential damages that result from the use or inability to use the software or related documentation, even if he has been advised of the possibility of such damages.

Table of Contents

Knowing Knoppix

Introducing Knoppix

*"Knoppix is... so astoundingly useful it's nearly
impossible to overpraise" — slashdot.org*

What is Knoppix?

Linux that runs from CD

Knoppix version 3.3 is an astonishingly clever product. It is a single CD that runs the
Linux *operating system* on your PC or laptop. An operating system is the base software
that makes a computer useful. Knoppix gives you a full graphical desktop with networking,
sound, the lot (subject to suitable hardware). No installation is necessary. Knoppix is
excellent for demonstrations, system recovery, or just testing how well the hardware in a
given PC is supported. The Knoppix CD is compressed. On-the-fly transparent
decompression gives a remarkable 1,600 Mb of software on a single 700 Mb CD.

How it works

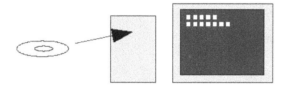

Start the computer using the Knoppix CD.

The existing software on the hard disk will be bypassed. The hard disk may still be accessed read-only. When you have finished using Knoppix, restart and take the CD out.
The regular operating system will run as normal.

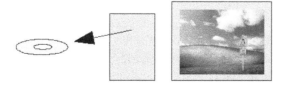

Safe to run

Knoppix leaves your existing software untouched. In fact, Knoppix can run on a computer with no hard disk at all! After running Knoppix, simply take the CD out of the drive. The computer will behave as if nothing has happened. The general philosophy of Knoppix is to access disks in read-only mode as much as possible. This is ideal for beginners, because it protects against accidents.

Personal

Settings and personal files can be saved to a disk, such a removable USB hard drive stick. This lets you store a personalised Knoppix setup and take it with you everywhere.

Free

Most amazing of all, Knoppix is free. The latest version is always available from the Knoppix download page. Not only is Knoppix free as in no charge, it is also free as in freedom. Subject to certain conditions, you are entitled to:

Make unlimited copies.
Use one copy on as many computers as you like.
Give unlimited copies to your friends.
Sell unlimited copies.
Customise it to suit yourself.
Redistribute your customised versions.

Web link

The Knoppix download page:
http://www.knoppix.net/

What you can do with Knoppix

Learn Linux

This book is designed to help you run Linux for the very first time. Knoppix is perfect for newcomers. Linux isn't going away any time soon. That is why learning it is an investment in your time that will pay off for years to come. This book is meant for people who are at least reasonably familiar with computers. For example, I assume you understand basic terms such as processor, motherboard, BIOS, RAM, CD-ROM, hard disk, USB, and soon. For definitions of computer and Internet terms, try Webopedia's online dictionary at `http://www.webopedia.com/`.

Rescue and test

Knoppix is a wonderful tool for rescuing and testing PCs. I will provide enough information to make Knoppix useful, without going into mindbending detail. With Knoppix it is possible to:

- Read files from Windows formatted hard disks, even when the operating system installed on the hard disk cannot be started (unless the hard disk has an unrecoverable data error, or if it is physically damaged).
- Copy files onto other disks, such as removable USB drives, Zip drives, CD-RW blanks and network drives (given suitable hardware).
- Identify hardware, even when Windows cannot identify it (subject to certain limitations).

Use and explore

Knoppix is a complete desktop system. Use it to:

- Print.
- Play sound.
- Use a scanner or a digital camera.
- Connect to the Internet.
- Browse the Internet's World Wide Web.
- Send and receive Internet email.
- Try out the built-in office applications, graphics tools, sound playing, video
- playing, Internet applications and games.

Network

Knoppix is a child of the Internet. Knoppix does networking with its eyes closed. For security reasons, Knoppix does not automatically run any servers that could be accessed from the outside.

Where Knoppix comes from

Knoppix was created in Germany by Klaus Knopper. Knoppix is a volunteer, cooperative, community effort. It exists entirely on the Internet. At the moment Knopper is the man who does most of the work on the disk. He does get patches and some scripts from the community, but he is still the most important person. The Knoppix project is hosted by LinuxTag, which is based in Germany at the Technical University of Kaiserslautern. The LinuxTag team runs conferences, workshops and exhibitions for everyone interested in Linux and Free Software.

> **Web links**
> The home page of Klaus Knopper:
> http://www.knopper.net/
> The home page of LinuxTag (in German):
> http://www.linuxtag.org/

Knoppix is Free Software

Knoppix is *Free Software*. It is licenced under the *GNU General Public Licence (GPL)*. Free Software is not freeware, and not shareware. Free Software means "free as in freedom", not necessarily price. This means you are allowed to run, copy, distribute, study, change and improve Knoppix at no charge. The catch is that when you give (or sell) copies to other people, you must give them the same freedoms under which you received it. This limitation ensures that Knoppix is free now and will remain free forever. For more details, see the licence text at the end of this book.

> **Web link**
> The Free Software Definition:
> http://www.gnu.org/philosophy/free-sw.html

Limitations

No warranty

Knoppix is experimental software. There is no warranty. Use at your own risk.

CD means slow

Compact Disc Read Only Memory (CD-ROM) drives are much slower than hard disk drives. This means that some applications on the Knoppix CD may take a long time to start; much longer than they would do on a full permanent Linux system. However, Knoppix has some clever (optional) tricks that can spectacularly speed things up. Knoppix does not get very far on unreliable CD-ROM drives. Since everything has to be loaded from CD, it falls over pretty quickly if CDROM errors occur, or if the Knoppix media itself is damaged. Knoppix has built-in tools for testing its own media.

Not everything works

Incompatible hardware includes: most internal dial-up and external USB broadband modems; AOL and Compuserve; certain low-cost inkjet printers; low-end colour laser printers; and most wireless (802.11b) network adapters. USB 2.0 is not supported which means that highspeed peripherals only work at the much slower USB 1.1 rate.Certain types of multimedia audio and video files are unplayable. Most commercial DVD movie discs cannot be played. In general, Knoppix does not run Windows soft-ware. Drag-and-drop or copy-and-paste between programs does not work, as a rule. User interface consistency is limited at best - behind Windows and not nearly as refined as the Apple Macintosh.

RAM intensive

The programs on the Knoppix CD have to be loaded into *RAM (Random Access Memory)* before they can be used. The more RAM you have, the better. For typical performance, you need 128 Mb RAM. If you are lucky enough to have 828 Mb RAM or more, Knoppix has clever tricks to make good use of all the RAM in your computer. This can deliver blazingly fast performance. If you have less than 128 Mb RAM, Knoppix has the ability to use part of the hard disk as if it were RAM. This is called creating a *swap file*. However, this does not work on all hard disks, and performance is much slower than real RAM.

What is included in Knoppix?

Knoppix is a compilation of a huge number of works from around the Internet. Some of the projects mentioned in this book are:

Project	Home page
AbiWord word processor	http://www.abisource.com/
Audacity sound recorder	http://audacity.sourceforge.net/
Common Unix Printing System (CUPS)	http://www.cups.org/
Gnumeric spreadsheet	http://www.gnumeric.org/
The GNU Image Manipulation Program (The Gimp)	http://www.gimp.org/
GNU utilities	http://www.gnu.org/
The K Desktop Environment (KDE)	http://www.kde.org/
Linux kernel	http://www.kernel.org/
Linux USB project	http://www.linux-usb.org/
Mozilla web browser	http://www.mozilla.org/
OpenOffice.org office suite	http://www.openoffice.org/
Samba file sharing server for Windows PCs	http://www.samba.org/
Scanner Access Is Now Easy (SANE)	http://www.sane-project.org/
Xine Media Player	http://xinehq.de/
X Multimedia System	http://www.xmms.org/
X Window System	http://www.xfree86.org/

Putting the above together and making sure it all works is the job of the *Debian* project (http://www.debian.org/). The result is called the Debian *distribution*. Knoppix is based on Debian, but with some special changes allowing it to run on a self-contained CD.

What is Linux?

Linux (pronounced "Lin-ucks") is the *kernel*. The kernel is the core component of the operating system. Think of an operating system as a nut. The *shell* is the part that you use. The kernel is the core that talks to the computer's hardware.

Note
There are many different Linux *distributions*. But there is only one current version of the Linux kernel. Therefore, every distribution contains Linux.

A little history

In the 1970s, computer *programs* were free. A program is a sequence of instructions that makes a "calculating machine" do something useful. The engineers who worked on these instructions became known as programmers. They shared their know-how with each other. They found that it made their work more pleasant.

Unfortunately, this cooperative spirit died under commercial pressures. Restrictive practices in the fast-growing "software industry" meant that sharing the most useful programs and some of the most vital technical information became largely impossible.

A man named Richard Stallman was greatly frustrated by this change. He wanted to bring back the spirit of the early days that he had known at MIT (Massachusetts Institute of Technology). He knew that he had the perfect skills to build a free operating system. He knew that if he didn't do it, no-one would. So he decided to do it, or "die trying".

By the 1990s, Stallman's *Free Software Foundation* had found or created nearly all the components of a free operating system. He called his creation "GNU Is Not UNIX".

The name is a joke designed to poke fun at the alphabet soup of computer acronyms. Some acronyms have other acronyms as part of their definition. The GNU acronym takes this one stage further - it has its own acronym as part of its definition. "Is Not" is a way of saying "is like" or "is compatible with".

UNIX refers to a family of operating systems that were used mainly in science, engineering and finance. Stallman chose to base his efforts on UNIX because it was tried and tested. It would also be convenient for other people to switch from UNIX to GNU.

How GNU grew

In 1991, the GNU project still lacked a kernel, the vital core component of an operating system. Luckily, a student in Finland called Linus Torvalds created one „as a hobby".

Linus Torvalds

In 1991, Torvalds produced a simple, basic system called "Freax". He called it "Linux" privately but never meant it to be called that in public, because he didn't want to be too egotistical. He made it free because he wanted feedback. It was posted on the Internet by a friend. Pretty soon, Torvalds began receiving email from places he'd dreamed of visiting, like Australia and the United States. Instead of cash, Linus preferred postcards. His sister Sara was suddenly impressed that her brother was somehow hearing from new friends far away.

Torvalds had used the Free Software Foundation's tools, so he decided to make it free likewise. This was a way to say îthank youî. He decided to put Linux under the Free Software Foundation's *General Public Licence*. This meant that anyone could use, improve or sell Linux, but no-one could take overall control.

It's a GNU world!

From there, it snowballed in the most extraordinary way. It has catapulted Torvalds to accidental super-stardom. He has appeared on the cover of Time magazine. However, we should remember that Stallman started it all. That is why Linux is correctly known in full as *GNU/Linux* - in other words, Knoppix is a Linux-based GNU system.

Web link
Overview and history of the GNU project:
http://www.gnu.org/gnu/gnu-history.html

Knoppix for the first time

*"The most important design issue... is that Linux is
supposed to be fun." — Linus Torvalds*

Overview

The purpose of this section is to get you started into Knoppix for the very first time. This section skips nearly all of the options for starting Knoppix. The options for starting Knoppix are explained later.

Hardware requirements

The recommended hardware is as follows:

> Intel Pentium compatible processor, 350 Mhz or faster.
> 128 Mb RAM or greater.
> Either: IDE or SCSI bootable CD-ROM drive
> Or: 3.5" floppy drive plus non-bootable CD-ROM drive.
> SVGA compatible graphics card (most cards supported).
> Monitor capable of 800x600 pixel resolution.
> Serial mouse, or PS/2 mouse, or USB mouse.

Starting Knoppix

There are two stages to starting Knoppix:

The first stage

The first stage is to get to the *boot prompt*. The boot prompt lets you customise the Knoppix startup process. For example, you can specify at the boot prompt what screen resolution you want Knoppix to use. To reach the boot prompt, you use either the CD or the floppy disk.

The second stage

The second stage is to run Knoppix itself. This requires the CD. Knoppix follows the instructions given at the boot prompt to complete the startup process.

The first stage

Getting to the boot prompt

To get to the boot prompt, follow these steps:

1. If the computer is already on, insert the Knoppix CD. If the CD drive is set to auto-run, information explaining about Knoppix will appear. Restart the computer.

2. If the computer is off, turn it on, then immediately insert the Knoppix CD. To play for time, press the Pause/Break key immediately after turning your computer on. On many PCs and laptops, this will pause the BIOS, giving you more time to insert the CD. Then press the Pause/Break key again to resume startup.

3. Most newer computers will automatically check for a bootable CD in the first CD-ROM drive. The Knoppix boot prompt should then appear. The boot prompt is the last three lines at the bottom of the screen. If your computer can't display the white and blue Knoppix logo, you will get a blue background instead.

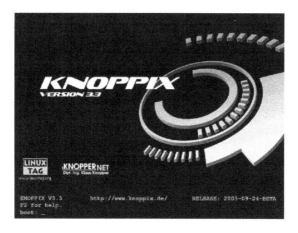

4. On some computers, you must press a key for the "boot device menu". The boot device menu is used to tell the computer which drive to boot from. A prompt saying which key will display the boot menu will appear on the screen just after you turn the computer on. For example, on some Dell desktop PCs, press F12 when prompted, press the Down Arrow key until "Boot from IDECDROM" is highlighted, then press Enter.

5. At the boot prompt, press Enter to boot Knoppix accepting all the defaults (including the German keyboard/language.) If you do nothing for 60 seconds, Knoppix boots automatically. To boot Knoppix with another keyboard/language, see the section "Which language?" below.

Tip

If you have two CD drives, and one of them is a CD Re-Writable drive, put the Knoppix CD in the other drive. Keep your writable drive empty if you can. This will let you try out the CD writing features in Knoppix easily at a later time.

Help at the boot prompt

Press F2 for the help screen. The help screen is a summary of the boot prompt options. Pressing F2 or any other key cancels the timer, so Knoppix will not automatically boot.

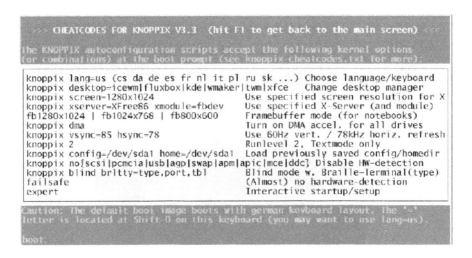

Quick help

Question: How do I get out of the boot prompt?
Take the CD out of the drive, then restart your computer.

Question: How do I use the boot floppy?

Turn off the computer. Insert the Knoppix boot floppy disk. Turn the computer back on. The computer should boot from the floppy drive. Then the Knoppix boot prompt should appear.

If that doesn't work, enter your computer's Basic In/Out System (BIOS) setup. The key to press that takes you into the BIOS setup is usually shown on the screen just after you turn the computer on. Visit the *boot priority* screen (it may have another name such as *boot device menu*). Set the BIOS to boot from the CD-ROM or floppy drive before the hard disk drive. If you do not know how to set the CD-ROM drive to boot first, check with your motherboard or computer manufacturer.

Question: The computer has two CD-ROM drives. Why does the Knoppix CD boot in one drive but not the other?

Some BIOSes can only boot the *first* CD-ROM drive. To work around the problem, start up from the Knoppix boot floppy disk. Then you can put the Knoppix CD in either CD-ROM drive. If you are really determined, switch the CD-ROM drive order so the drive you want to boot from is the first drive.

The second stage

Starting Knoppix proper

To start Knoppix with the United Kingdom keyboard/language:
1. Type this at the boot prompt:
    ```
    knoppix lang=uk
    ```
2. Press the Enter key on the keyboard.
3. Knoppix will begin loading with the UK keyboard/language.

Which keyboard/language?

The most important option at the boot prompt is the keyboard/language. More correctly, the keyboard/language option sets the *locale*. A locale is a collection of regional settings including keyboard layout, language, time format, date format, currency format and paper size. Some language translations may be incomplete. The locale options are named using the International Standards Organisation two-letter country codes (ISO 3166 and ISO 639). The locale options are:

Code	Keyboard/language
de	German (default)
be	Belgian
bg	Bulgarian
ch	Swiss
cn	Simplified Chinese
cs or cz	Czech
dk or da	Dansk
es	Spanish

Code	Keyboard/language
fi	Finnish (incomplete)
fr	French
he or il	Hebrew
it	Italian
jp	Japanese (limited)
nl	Dutch
pl	Polish
ru	Russian
sl	Slovakian (guessed)
tr	Turkish
tw	Traditional Chinese
uk	United Kingdom
us	United States

Automatic hardware detection

Knoppix will then try to detect the various items of hardware in your computer. How long it takes depends upon the speed of your machine. Here are some examples to give you an idea of what to expect:

Processor	RAM	CD-ROM speed	Time needed
Intel Pentium 4 (2.6 Ghz)	512 Mb	48x	40 seconds
AMD Duron (1 Ghz)	256 Mb	32x	45 seconds
AMD Athlon (600 Mhz)	128 Mb	24x 1	min 30 seconds

The X Window System

Next, it will briefly say "INIT: Entering runlevel 5" and then Knoppix will try to start the *X Window System*. The X Window System is the graphics display. If you have a supported graphics card, you will see a black cross on a grey stippled background. This means the X Window System started successfully.

The K Desktop Environment

Knoppix will begin loading the *K Desktop Environment*. KDE runs on top of the X Window System. The progress of loading KDE will be shown in the middle of the screen. When KDE has finished loading, the welcome page will be loaded. When the welcome page appears, congratulations! You have started Linux, the X Window System, and the K Desktop Environment successfully.

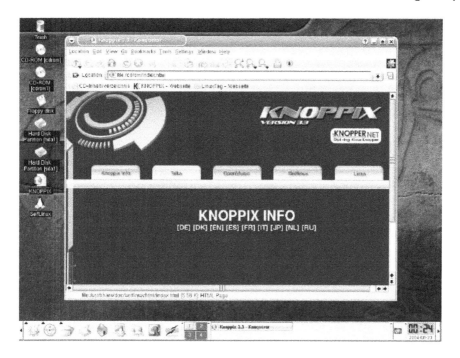

Quick help

Question: Why does KDE come up in German?

You need to specify the keyboard/language at the boot prompt. For example, for the UK locale, enter `knoppix lang=uk` at the boot prompt.

Question: It says 'cloop: read error', what does that mean?

There is a problem reading the Knoppix CD. You either have a faulty CD-ROM drive or a damaged CD. To test the Knoppix CD, enter at the boot prompt :

```
knoppix testcd
```

This will make Knoppix check the media for errors. If you know that the Knoppix CD is good, this error usually means a faulty CD-ROM drive.

Question: I get a blank screen when the X Window System comes up, why?

Knoppix is trying to use a screen resolution that your monitor doesn't support. For example, Knoppix may have detected your graphics card is capable of 1024x768 pixel resolution, but your monitor can't cope with that. Try setting a lower resolution at the boot prompt. For example, enter:

```
knoppix lang=uk screen=800x600
```

This will make Knoppix use a screen resolution of 800 by 600 pixels when it starts the X Window System.

Question: Why does the screen go blank when the kernel boots?

This problem usually occurs with low cost TFT (flat screen) monitors. The kernel is using a framebuffer console, but the monitor is incompatible with it. Turn off the framebuffer console. At the boot prompt, use the option vga=normal. For example, type:

```
knoppix lang=uk vga=normal
```

This will turn off the framebuffer console and the penguin logo.

Question: Why doesn't the mouse work?

This could mean you are trying to use a PS/2 mouse in a 9-pin serial port through a PS/2-to-serial adapter. Some PS/2 mice do not work when plugged into a 9-pin serial port. Try a real serial mouse.

Question: It says "Initrd extends beyond end of memory".

Your motherboard is reporting the RAM size incorrectly. Specify the amount of physical RAM in your computer at the boot prompt. For example, if you have 128 Mb of RAM, enter at the boot prompt:

```
knoppix lang=uk mem=128M
```

Question: It says "Could not find the KNOPPIX filesystem, sorry. Dropping you to a (very limited) shell."

Try booting with:

```
knoppix ide2=0x180 nopcmcia
```

If that doesn't work, it means your PCMCIA CD-ROM drive is not supported. There is a workaround. In Windows, copy the directory called ìKNOPPIXî from the Knop-pix CD to the root of a local FAT formatted hard drive partition (eg: drive ìC:î). The copy will take some time to complete. Then start Knoppix and specify the partition that you copied the KNOPPIX directory to, using the `fromhd=` boot parameter. For example, boot with:

```
knoppix fromhd=/dev/hda1
```

If Windows is not available, use a single-floppy Linux such as "tomsrtbt" to do the copy, however that is beyond the scope of this book.

Getting out

Now that you've got Knoppix up and running, feel free to have a poke around. Everything is read-only, so you're unlikely to do any harm to your computer. To exit Knoppix:

1. Click the "K" menu in the bottom left corner.
2. Click "Logout".

3. Knoppix will begin shutting down.
4. The Knoppix CD will be ejected.
5. Remove the CD and close the tray.
6. Press Enter on the keyboard.
7. Knoppix will attempt to turn off the computer automatically. If it doesn't turn off automatically, it is now safe to turn off the computer yourself using the power button.

Tip

For a quick exit, press Ctrl+Alt+Backspace. This "three finger salute" kills the X Window System. Killing the X Window System takes down KDE and all its open applications. Knoppix will then shut down automatically.

The K Desktop Environment

The *K Desktop Environment* is a modern, powerful and free graphical user interface environment for UNIX compatible systems. Its name is a play on the *Common Desktop Environment* created by Sun Microsystems in the 1980s. This section explains what KDE has to offer.

Web link
The home page of the K Desktop Environment:
http://www.kde.org/

Single click, not double-click

KDE looks familiar to Windows and Macintosh users because it takes some of the best elements from each. There is an important difference: everything is single click. Nothing needs a double-click to make it work. If you double-click, you'll end up with a program running twice, or something else you don't need. Just single click.

Tip
To select a file instead of opening it, hold down the Ctrl key and click the left mouse button. The icon will be selected, rather than opened. It is then safe to let go of the Ctrl key.

Context menus everywhere

Most icons have a context menu. To get the context menu for an icon, right-click on the icon.

> **Tip**
> Right-click to see the context menu for an item.

Hover the mouse for help

Like Macintosh and Windows, most icons have a tooltip. Hover the mouse pointer over an icon. A little yellow label will tell you what that icon does.

Tooltips only work in the current active window. This means that if you have two windows open, you will only get tooltips in the window that is at the front. To get tooltips in the other window, you must click it to bring it to the front.

> **Tip**
> Not sure what an icon does? Hover the mouse pointer over it.

The Desktop

The main part of the screen is called the *Desktop*. This is where the application windows appear. There are also icons for each *disk device* in the system. Here are device icons for two CD-ROM drives, a 1.44 Mb floppy drive, and a hard disk partition. Notice that the "hard disk partition" icon has the name "hda1". Knoppix has its own way of naming disks and partitions. For details, see the section "Knoppix essentials".

These icons are actually hyperlinks. In other words, they are just pointers to the place in the system where the files appear. You can't drag and drop files and folders onto Desktop device icons, as you can on the Apple Macintosh.

Note

Desktop icons are shortcuts. There are no files inside Desktop icons. Instead, Desktop icons are just pointers to the places where the files actually appear.

If you plug in a hot-pluggable disk device, such as a USB external hard drive, a new icon for it will appear on the Desktop. This behaviour will be familiar to Apple Macintosh users.

The Panel

At the bottom of the screen is the *Panel*. The Panel is always visible. It contains various utilities and status information.

K Menu

In the far left corner of the Panel is the *K Menu* which is just like theWindows "Start" menu. Click for a list of programs that are available on the system.

Quick launch

Next to the K Menu are *Quick Launch* icons. These icons represent frequently used programs.

Hover the mouse pointer over the program icon for a description of what it does. Single-click on the icon to start that program. Be aware that the *OpenOffice* program may take several minutes to start, especially if you have a slower computer.

Desktop Guide

The *Desktop Guide* consists of four squares. Each square represents one desktop. You start off in the first desktop. Click in the Desktop Guide to switch between the four available desktops.

To move open windows between Desktops, click the Window Control Box at the top left corner of the window. Point at "To desktop", then choose the Desktop that you would like to send the window to.

Taskbar

A button is shown in the *Taskbar* for each open window. This example shows three open windows; *Konsole*, the *Konqueror* web browser, and the *GIMP* graphics editor.

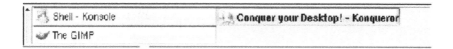

System Tray

The *System Tray* contains an icon for the current keyboard layout. To view the avai-lable keyboard layouts, right-click on the keyboard layout icon.

Clock

The clock shows the time and date.

Hide Panel

At each end of the Panel is a *Hide Panel* button. Click the Hide Panel button to make the Panel shrink to that side of the screen. Click the button again to unhide the Panel. Drag the Hide Panel button to move the entire Panel from one side of the screen to another.

Left mouse button selects text, middle button pastes

To copy and paste text using a three button mouse:

1. Select the text that you want to copy and paste with the left mouse button, so that the text is highlighted.
2. Point to the place where you want the text to go.
3. Click the middle mouse button. The last selected text will be pasted from the X Window System's *copy buffer* into the place where you clicked.

Knoppix essentials

"If I ever met Bill Gates, there wouldn't be much of a
meeting point. I couldn't tell him about business, and
he couldn't tell me about technology."
— Linus Torvalds

This section contains important background information that will help you understand the rest of this book. If you are in a hurry, skip over this section. The terms explained in this section will be used often, so you may need to refer back to this page later.

File names

The following rules apply to file names in Knoppix.

Case sensitive. This causes the most problems for beginners. For example, "myfile.txt", "MyFile.txt" and "MYFILE.TXT" are all different names.

Long file names are allowed. File names can be up to 255 characters long.

There is no "C:" drive. Instead, all files are arranged in a tree beginning with "/", which is called the *root directory*. The "root directory" is like "My Computer". It is the starting point for everything stored inside in the computer.

Forward slashes. For example, in Windows, part of the location of an image file might be:

```
My Documents\My Pictures\duck.jpg
```

In Knoppix, the backslashes that represent the path to the file are written as forward slashes instead, like this:

```
My Documents/My Pictures/duck.jpg
```

> **Note**
> What's the difference between a directory and a folder? Not much. A folder is just the icon that is usually used to represent a directory. The words "directory" and "folder" are interchangable. Remember, a hard disk is like a filing cabinet. Partitions are like drawers, directories are like folders, and files are like individual documents.

Drive names

You may be used to Microsoft Windows' naming scheme for disk drives. For example, you may be used to "drive A:" for the first floppy drive; "drive C:" for the first visible hard drive partition, and so on. Knoppix has its own drive naming scheme. This section explains how the naming scheme works.

Disk types

The naming scheme starts with a two-letter code for the type of disk.

Name	Drive type
fd	Conventional floppy drive
hd	Integrated Drive Electronics (IDE) drive
sd	Small Computer System Interface (SCSI) drive

IDE drives

IDE drives are the most common in desktop PCs and laptops. A single letter indicates how the drive is connected. Most PCs and laptops have two IDE *channels*: primary and secondary. Each channel can have up to two devices: master and slave.

Name	IDE drive
hda	Primary Master
hdb	Primary Slave
hdc	Secondary Master
hdd	Secondary Slave

SCSI drives

For SCSI drives, a single letter indicates its location. This is called its position in the *SCSI chain*. SCSI hard drives are usually found in servers. Zip, USB and Firewire drives are also treated as SCSI drives.

Name	SCSI drive location
sda	First SCSI drive
sdb	Second SCSI drive
sdc	Third SCSI drive

Disk partitions

IDE and SCSI hard drives are divided into *partitions*. Zip, USB and Firewire drives also contain partitions. A partition is like a compartment within a disk. There may be a single partition that covers the entire disk. There may be more than one partition. Each partition is indicated by a number.

Name	Drive	Partition
hda1	Primary master IDE drive	First partition
hda2	Primary master IDE drive	Second partition
hda3	Primary master IDE drive	Third partition

SCSI emulation for IDE CD-ROM drives

IDE CD-ROM drives are treated as SCSI drives. This is called *SCSI emulation*. SCSI emulation is there so that CD burning applications can use the same language to talk to SCSI and IDE drives.

Name	CD-ROM drive
scd0	First CD-ROM drive
scd1	Second CD-ROM drive
scd2	Third CD-ROM drive

Conventional 1.44 Mb floppy drives

For ordinary floppy disk drives, a number shows the drive number.

Name	Floppy drive number
fd0	First floppy drive
fd1	Second floppy drive

Partition detection

Knoppix automatically detects all partitions on all IDE and SCSI devices. For example, given a single Windows partition on the primary master IDE hard drive, the following *device name* will be created:

```
/dev/hda1
```

This means the partition will be called /dev/hda1 in Knoppix.

> **Note**
>
> Some removable disks also have partitions, notably Iomega Zip disks. For the partitions on an Iomega Zip disk to be detected properly, you must insert the disk into the drive before you start Knoppix.

Mount points

Each device name has a *mount point*. This is a special place where the files on a device appear. A mount point is created automatically for each device name. For example, given the Fujitsu drive above, the following mount point will be created:

```
/mnt/hda1
```

This means the partition `/dev/hda1` will be mounted to `/mnt/hda1`.

Auto-mounting of floppy and CD-ROM drives

Conventional floppy and CD-ROM drives are *auto-mounted*. This means Knoppix takes care of mounting and unmounting them automatically. The auto-mount locations are:

First floppy drive:	`/mnt/floppy`
Second floppy drive:	`/mnt/floppy1`
First CD-ROM drive:	`/mnt/cdrom`
Second CD-ROM drive:	`/mnt/cdrom1`

Login accounts

When you start Knoppix, you are logged in automatically. No passwords are needed. All passwords are locked by default. Knoppix bypasses all the usernames and passwords of the operating system installed on the hard disk.

Keyboard shortcut	Virtual terminal	Logged in as user account
Ctrl+Alt+F1	Console number 1	root
Ctrl+Alt+F2	Console number 2	root
Ctrl+Alt+F3	Console number 3	root
Ctrl+Alt+F4	Console number 4	root
Ctrl+Alt+F5	X Window System (KDE)	knoppix

You can switch between the virtual terminals at any time. For example, to switch to the first console, press Ctrl+Alt+F1. The Knoppix startup messages will be displayed. To switch to the second console, press Ctrl+Alt+F2. To get back to the X Window System, press Ctrl+Alt+F5.

Note

The X Window System is on virtual terminal number 5.

User accounts

The user account

The Knoppix *user* account is called "knoppix". This account is for all productivity tasks, including CD burning and printing. When the X Window System starts, you are logged in to that user account automatically, without a password.

The superuser account

The *superuser* account is for system administration tasks. The superuser account is called the root *account*. When Knoppix starts, you are logged in as *root* to all four consoles automatically with no password. It is also possible to use the root account within the X Window System.

Important

As with other Linux distributions, use the *user* account for all your everyday tasks. Only use the *root account* when you need it. For example, when you are logged on as *root*, you have the power to instantly delete every file on every disk with one simple command. When you are logged on as a *user*, the system will not let you do that. This helps you to protect yourself against accidents. Get into the habit now and it will save you later!

Identifying hardware

Knoppix has built-in hardware identification. This means Knoppix can identify the make and model of a huge range of common PC components, such as processors, graphics cards, network cards, and so on. To use the hardware identification:

1. Click K Menu.
2. Click System.
3. Click Info Center.

4. The *Info Center* application will come up. On the left side are the various categories. Click a category to view the details.

   The most useful categories are:

   > Processor (Central Processing Unit).
   > Memory (Random Access Memory, or RAM).
   > Partitions (partitions on hard disks and other drives).
   > PCI (Peripheral Component Interconnect cards).
   > PCMCIA (credit-card sized cards for laptops. PCMCIA stands for
   >   Personal Computer Manufacturer Interface Adapter).
   > Storage Devices (hard disks and other drives).
   > USB Devices (Universal Serial Bus peripherals).

Note

If you plug in a new USB device, and you are already on the USB Devices page, choose any other category and then select USB Devices again to refresh the list.

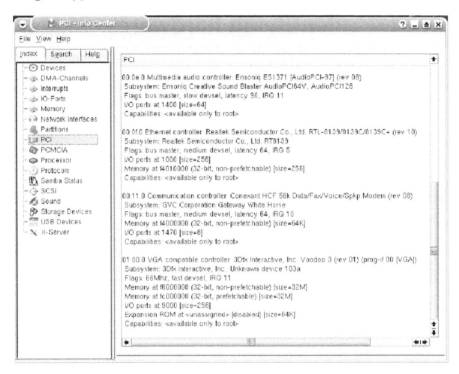

Listing hard disks

To get a listing of the hard disk drives in the computer, including the make and model of each one:

1. Click the Konsole (bottom row, 6th from the left).

2. Enter the following command, then press Enter.
   ```
   dmesg
   ```

3. The dmesg command shows the "kernel messages". You will get quite a lot of output. Scroll up about two-thirds of the way until you see lines like this:

```
hda: ST320410A, ATA DISK drive
hdc: JLMS XJ-HD165H, ATAPI CD/DVD-ROM drive
hdd: LITE-ON LTR-52327S, ATAPI CD/RW drive
```

The example above is from a computer with IDE drives. It has one hard disk drive and two CD drives. The primary master (hda) is a "Seagate Technology 320410A" hard disk drive. "ATA" stands for „AT Attachment". The secondary master (hdc) is a DVD drive and the secondary slave (hdd) is a CD writer.

> **Tip**
> To see only the lines from `dmesg` that contain the letters "hd", enter:
> `dmesg | grep hd`
> The "|" character is a vertical bar, not a capital "i". On a UK keyboard layout, the vertical bar is on the key between "Z" and the left "Shift".

Limitations

The ability to identify hardware is tremendously useful. However, there are limitations you should know about.

Hardware newer than itself

The most important limitation is that Knoppix cannot accurately identify PCI and PCMCIA hardware newer than itself. USB and Firewire devices work differently and are not subject to this limitation. This book comes with Knoppix version 3.3, which is dated September 2003. Knoppix should be able to identify most hardware made before then (except the very old or very rare). However, Knoppix version 3.3 may only be able to identify PCI and PCMCIA hardware made after September 2003 as an "Unknown device". A newer version of Knoppix may help. A newer version can be ob-tained from the Knoppix web site and from other vendors.

Winmodems

A *winmodem* is a modem that relies on Windows software to make it work. This is done to save a few components and reduce manufacturing costs. For this reason, winmodems tend not to work well with Knoppix. A common example is the Intel 537 series of PCI internal modem cards. Knoppix can only tell you what a winmodem identifies itself as, in its hardware. Knoppix cannot tell you about the Windows-specific software needed to get it working in Windows. For example, in the case of Intel 537 based winmodems, there are many different vendor-specific Windows drivers, which may be incompatible with each other. However, these cards will all be reported the same in Knoppix. That is more a limitation of the hardware, rather than a limitation of Knoppix.

Identified does not mean supported

Knoppix may not have driver support for all the hardware it can identify. In other words, just because Knoppix tells you the make and model of a device does not mean it actually works in Knoppix. For example, the Intel 536EP internal modem PCI card is accurately identified; but it is not usable because it requires proprietary software that cannot be distributed with Knoppix.

Not guaranteed

The identification provided by Knoppix may be wrong. This is because Knoppix is not perfect (sorry). However, it is pretty reliable. For example, in two years of using Knoppix every day, I have had only one instance of wrongly identified hardware (a fairly obscure sound card). The hardware identification strings are mostly provided by Linux users, rather than the hardware vendors themselves. However, the hardware vendors are not perfect either. Sometimes the Linux users' identification corrects mistakes made by hardware vendors!

Reading the hard disk

Knoppix supports all IDE and most SCSI hard disk drives. It reads files from the full range of Microsoft operating systems - from MS-DOS through to Windows XP.

This is useful because if you cannot start Windows, often all the data files are still there happily on the hard disk. On many occasions, it is a simple matter to locate the files using Knoppix. It is usually then equally trivial to rescue the files by copying them somewhere safe (explained in the later sections).

To browse the files on the internal hard disk, look on the Desktop. You should see an icon for each hard disk partition. To access the files on that partition:

1. Click the icon for the hard disk partition.
2. Wait for a moment while the partition is mounted. A green triangle will appear, indicating that the partition is in use.

3. Wait while the Konqueror file manager starts up.
4. The files on the partition should be displayed, read only. This example shows a typical "drive C:" from a computer that usually runs Windows 98.

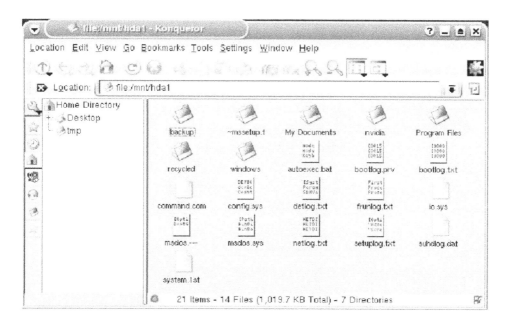

Selecting files and folders

To create data CDs and copy files and folders onto other disks, you need to know how to select. There are several ways to select files and folders:

Lasoo. Click and hold the left mouse button on a blank area in the Konqueror window. Drag across to the opposite corner. The files and folders in the marked area will be selected. To unselect, click any blank area within the window.

Ctrl + click. Hold down the Ctrl key on the keyboard, and click a file or folder. It will be selected. To unselect, Ctrl + click the file or folder icon again, or click any blank area within the window.

Shift + click. Ctrl + click the first file or folder. Let go of the Ctrl Key. Hold down the Shift key, and select the last file or folder. The range will be selected. To unselect, click any blank area within the window.

Right-click. Click the right hand mouse button on a file or folder. A "context menu" will appear, showing the most common actions for that item. The file or folder will also be selected. To unselect, click any blank area within the window.

Enabling write access

Knoppix has the optional ability to write to hard disk drives. *Write mode* lets you copy files to the drive, and change existing files. Knoppix supports writing to MS-DOS and Windows 95/98/Me formatted partitions. Writing to native Windows NT/2000/XP partitions is not supported. To enable write access:

1. Click the icon of the hard disk partition you want to write to.
2. Wait for a moment while the partition is mounted.
3. Wait while the Konqueror file manager starts up.
4. The files on the partition will be displayed.
5. Right-click the icon of the hard disk partition.
6. Click "Change read/write mode".

7. You will be prompted to make the partition writable. Click "Yes".

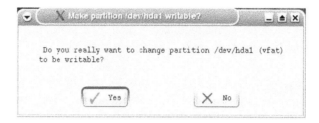

8. You should now be able to write files to the partition.

Quick help

Question: There are no icons for the hard disk on the Desktop.

If you have an IDE hard disk, this usually means the BIOS did not detect the hard disk drive. Go into your motherboard's BIOS and make sure the hard disk is detected by the BIOS properly. If you have one of the recent "Serial ATA" hard drives, they are not supported in Knoppix version 3.3. You need Knoppix version 3.6 or later.

Question: I still can't access the hard disk.

The partition may be encrypted, which means it may have been specially set up on purpose to make it inaccessible to outside tools like Knoppix. The partition table may be incorrect, or there may be data errors. In the worst case, the drive may be physically damaged; listen for ping-pong ball bouncing or loud rattling noises.

Question: How can I check or test my hard disk?

Knoppix has many built-in tools, but they are beyond the scope of this book. You will need a more advanced book, a knowledgeable friend or help online to use these tools. Having said that, here is a hint. To list the commands that have the words "dos", "ntfs" or "partition" anywhere in their short description, enter:

```
man -k dos ntfs partition
```

CD writing

Knoppix has built-in support for CD writing. To create your own CDs using Knoppix, it is best to have two CD drives. You need one drive for the Knoppix CD, and a Compact Disc Re-Writable drive for the blank media. Normally, the Knoppix CD occupies the first drive, and it cannot be removed while Knoppix is running.

However, if you have a suitable hard disk, it is possible to start Knoppix from a single CD-ROM drive and then use it for other CDs. See the later section, "Advanced startup options".

The following CD-RW drives are compatible with Knoppix:

All SCSI CD-RW drives.
Nearly all IDE CD-RW drives produced after 1999.
Some IDE CD-RW drives produced before 1999.
Most external (USB) CD-RW drives.

Knoppix uses SCSI commands to create CDs. When working with IDE CD-RW drives, Knoppix uses SCSI *emulation*. This means that Knoppix works with IDE CD-RW drives while actually using the SCSI language to talk to the drive. For this reason, SCSI CD-RW drives are ideal, while most IDE CD-RW drives should work. To copy files onto a data CD:

1. Select the files or folders to be written onto CD.
2. Right-click on the selection.
3. Click "Create CD with K3b".
4. Wait for a moment while the *K3b* program starts.

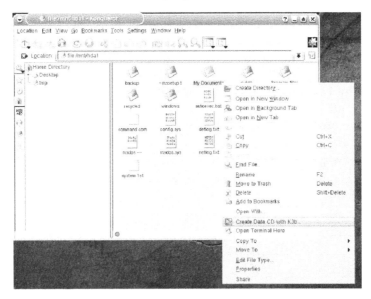

5. The K3b window will be displayed. In the "Current Projects" pane, you will see the folder that you chose. To add additional files and folders, drag and drop them into the Project pane.

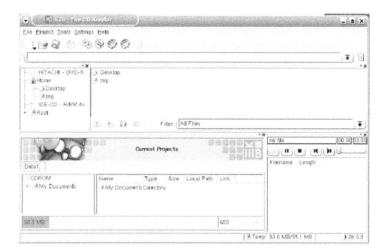

6. The disk usage is in shown in the green bar at the bottom of the Projects pane. It shows the amount of space that will be used on the writable CD. This example shows 90.3 Mb will be used, out of a possible 650 Mb.

7. Click the "Burn" button (fourth from the left in the toolbar). The disk writing window will be appear. The make and model of your CD-RW drive will be shown.

8. Select the writing speed to be used from the ìSpeedî box. The correct writing speed to choose depends upon the speed of your CDRW drive and the media. For example, if you have an 8x CD-RW drive and 4-10x compatible media, choose 8x.

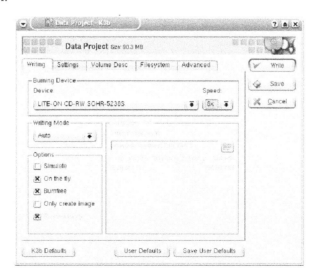

9. Click the "Filesystem" tab.

10. Click "Generate Joliet extensions" to put a tick in the box. This step is needed to make the CD fully readable in Windows. If you are only going to use the CD in another Linux or UNIX computer, you do not need this.

11. Click "Write".

12. The CD will be created. When the writing process has finished, the CD will be ejected.

13. Click "Close" to return to K3b.

Quick help

Question: Why does it eject the CD and do nothing? Or, why do I get an error while CD writing?

You may be trying to use incompatible media. For example, if you try to write onto CD-RW media labelled "4-10x compatible" at 32x then the drive will just eject the blank CD.

Question: When I put the written CD in a computer running Windows, some of the file names come out in capitals and some spaces or dots are turned into underscores. Why?

You need step 10, "Generate Joliet extensions". The original specification for data CDs allows each file name only 8 characters plus a 3 character extension. For example: "hello.txt" fits, but "long file name of your dreams.txt" does not. "Joliet" is the Microsoft way of putting long file names on a data CD.

Reading CD-ROMs

Knoppix has built-in support for reading *Compact Disc Digital Data* discs. It is best to have two CD drives - one for the Knoppix CD, and one for the data CD that you want to read. If not, see "If you have only one CD drive" in the "Advanced startup options" section. To read a data CD:

1. Insert the data CD into an empty CD-ROM drive.
2. Click the icon on the Desktop on that represents the drive. The "CDROM" icon represents the first CD drive, and "CDROM1" represents the second drive.
3. A green triangle will appear on the CD drive icon to indicate that the drive is in use.
4. Wait while the Konqueror file manager starts up.
5. The files on the CD will be displayed.

Ejecting the CD

1. Close all windows and files opened from the CD.
2. Press the Eject button on the front of the drive.
3. The CD tray will be ejected.

Quick help

Question: When trying to access a CD for the first time, it says "The file or directory file:/mnt/cdrom does not exist". What does this mean?

Usually this means the drive is still preparing itself, or the Knoppix auto-mounter has not finished working yet. Wait a few moments, then try again. If it still doesn't work, click the Home icon in the Panel, then type `file:/mnt/auto/cdrom` or `file:/mnt/auto/cdrom1`. If it still doesn't work, click the Knoppix icon in the Panel, click Root Shell, then enter this command: `/etc/init.d/autofs restart`.

Question: Why is the CD stuck in the drive?

Knoppix uses the locking mechanism of the drive to prevent you from taking out a CD that is still in use. Close all windows and documents opened from the CD, then try again.

Question: When I right-click on the CD drive's icon and then click "Eject", it says "Eject failed!" What does that mean?

It means the drive doesn't like the Knoppix "eject" program. Just press the eject button on the front of the drive instead.

Using an external USB drive

Knoppix supports two types of external USB hard drive:

USB hard drive stick (also known as flash or pen drive).
Conventional external USB hard disk drive.

Knoppix uses its built-in *USB Mass Storage* driver to support these drives. USB 1.1 and USB 2.0 drives are supported, **but** USB 2.0 drives only work at USB 1.1 speed in Knoppix version 3.3.

Note
USB 1.1 works at up to 12 megabits per second (about 1.5 megabytes per second). USB 2.0 allows up to 480 megabits per second (about 60 megabytes per second) when plugged into a USB 2.0 capable socket – but this is not available in Knoppix version 3.3. If you need USB 2.0 at its highest speed, use Knoppix version 3.6 or later and start with `knoppix usb2` at the boot prompt.

A USB hard drive stick is a small device like a key fob. Many digital cameras also work as an external USB hard drive. Any digital camera that supports USB Mass Storage should work. Some cameras need to be put into "DSC Mode" to enable USB Mass Storage. To copy files onto an external USB hard disk drive:

1. Insert the USB drive into any USB socket.
2. After a short pause, an icon for each partition on the new drive should appear. In most cases there will be a single partition on the USB drive that covers the entire disk, so one new icon will appear. If the icon doesn't appear, take the USB drive out and insert it again more slowly. There are four pins on the USB drive's connector. Two of the four pins are longer because they must make contact first.

    To see if Knoppix accepts the USB drive when you put it in, refer to the "Identifying Hardware" section. Look at the Info Center's "USB Devices" and „Storage Devices" categories.

3. When USB drive icon appears, click it with the left mouse button.
4. Wait for a moment while it is mounted.
5. The files on the USB drive will be displayed.
6. Right-click the icon of the USB drive.
7. Click "Change read-write mode".
8. Click "Yes".

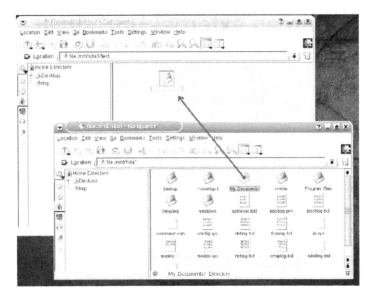

9. Drag and drop the files or folders that you want to copy into the window of the USB drive.
10. Click "Copy Here".

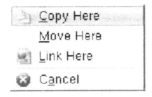

11. The files or folders will be copied.
12. When copying has finished, close all open windows for the USB drive.
13. Right-click on the icon of the USB drive.
14. Click "Unmount".
15. The green triangle on the USB drive's icon will go away.
16. It is now safe to take the USB drive out of its socket.

Quick help

Question: Why is my USB 2.0 drive slow?

USB 2.0 drives only work at USB 1.1 speed in Knoppix version 3.3. Use Knoppix 3.6 or later and start with `knoppix usb2` at the boot prompt.

Question: I can't get my USB drive to appear.

Click Konsole, then type `dmesg`. If the drive is connected successfully, you will see lines like this at or near the end of the output:

```
scsi2 : SCSI emulation for USB Mass Storage devices
   Vendor: USB2.0 Model: Flash Disk Rev: 2.00
   Type: Direct-Access ANSI SCSI revision: 02
Attached scsi removable disk sda at scsi2
SCSI device sda: 512000 512-byte hdwr sectors (262 MB)
sda: Write Protect is off
   sda: sda1
```

This shows that a "USB2.0 Flash Disk" has appeared as the first SCSI drive (sda). It is 262 Mb in size. It contains one partition (sda1). If you insert a USB drive too quickly, it will say "unable to read partition table" instead of "SCSI device". This means try again, more slowly.

If it still won't work, run `dmesg` to find out why. Look for messages like

```
   sda: I/O error
```
or
```
   sda: Device reports illegal request.
```

Test it with Windows or MacOS. If it works there, it may mean the device is non-standard or it has special needs. The Linux kernel has built-in workarounds for "unusual devices", but this lags behind in time after new USB devices come out. Try a newer version of Knoppix. In the last resort, try another USB drive. Go to the Linux USB home page:

```
   http://www.linux-usb.org/
```

Click "Working Device List" and then "Mass Storage". This will tell you which devices work and which do not.

Question: Why did it say "out of disk space" while copying, even though the total size of the files to be copied is less than the free space on the drive?

Some USB drives are formatted with the FAT12 or FAT16 filesystem. This is inefficient when storing small files. If there are many small files, the drive may fill up much more quickly that you might expect. There are two ways round the problem. The first way is to archive the files onto the flash drive. To archive means to create one big file instead of lots of small ones. To create an archive, click K menu, Utilities, Ark (Archiving Tool). The second way is to reformat the drive to a more efficient file-system, such as FAT32.

Using a 3.5" floppy drive

Knoppix supports all standard 1.44 Mb floppy drives. If you have an Imation LS120 SuperDisk drive, see the later section. The SuperDisk drive is not a standard 1.44 Mb floppy drive; it works quite differently.

To copy files onto a 3.5" floppy drive:

1. Check the write-protect tab on the floppy disk. Make sure the tab is in the closed (write enabled) position.
2. Insert the floppy disk into the drive.
3. Click once on the "Floppy Disk" icon on the Desktop.
4. The files on the floppy will be displayed.
5. Drag and drop files and folders to be copied into the floppy disk window.
6. Click "Copy Here".
7. The files will be copied.
8. Wait until the floppy drive's "busy" light goes out.
9. Close the floppy disk window.
10. It is now safe to remove the floppy disk from the drive.

Note

Unmounting a 3.5" floppy disk is done for you automatically. There is no need to "Change read-write mode", because the read-write tab on the floppy disk itself controls whether it is writable or not.

Quick help

Question: How do I format a 3.5" floppy?

Right-click the "Floppy disk" icon on the Desktop, then click "Format Floppy disk".

Question: I have an Imation SuperDisk floppy drive. Why does clicking on the Floppy icon not do anything?

The Imation SuperDisk is not an ordinary floppy drive. It is treated as a hard disk drive. Follow the instructions in the Imation LS-120 SuperDisk section.

Using an Iomega Zip disk

The Iomega Zip disk drive was very popular in the 1990s. It has been somewhat superseded by the CD-RW and the USB flash drive. However, Iomega Zip drives, and their media, are still easy to find and often useful. The usual capacity of Iomega Zip media is 100 or 250 Mb.

There are three varieties of Iomega Zip drive: internal, parallel, and USB. The internal and parallel varieties are older and are no longer made. The USB variety is newer and is still being made today.

Note

Iomega measures its disk capacities in megabytes where 1 megabyte = one million bytes. This is less than the conventional definition where 1 megabyte = 1,048,576 bytes. Knoppix uses the conventional definition. Therefore a "Zip 100" disk has an actual capacity of 98,078 kilobytes according to Knoppix.

Using an external USB Iomega Zip drive

The external USB Iomega Zip drive is available in 100 Mb, 250 Mb and 750 Mb versions. The 750 Mb version also supports USB 2.0 for higher transfer speeds. Knoppix uses its built-in USB Mass Storage driver to support the external USB Iomega Zip drive. To copy files onto an external USB Iomega Zip drive:

1. With the computer off, plug the Zip drive into a USB socket.
2. Insert a valid PC formatted Zip disk into the drive.
3. Start Knoppix, but specify text mode at the command prompt. For example, enter:
   ```
   knoppix lang=uk dma 2
   ```
4. Knoppix will start up, but then stop before loading KDE.
5. Press Enter on the keyboard to wake up the command prompt. Type this command, then press Enter:
   ```
   rebuildfstab -u knoppix -g knoppix
   ```
6. You should see the activity light on the front of the drive come on, and you should hear the drive work.
7. Switch to graphics mode with this command:
   ```
   init 5
   ```
8. After KDE loads, you will see an icon for the Zip drive on the Desktop. Assuming you have no other SCSI drives, the icon will be labelled "Hard disk partition [sda4]".
9. Click the icon for the Zip drive.

10. Wait while the device is mounted.
11. Wait while the "Konqueror" file manager starts up.
12. The files on the Zip disk will be displayed.
13. Right-click the Zip drive's icon.
14. Click "Change read/write mode".
15. Click "Yes".
16. Drag and drop the files and folders to be copied into the Zip disk's window.
17. Click „"Copy Here".
18. The files and folders will be copied.
19. Close all the Zip disk's open windows.
20. Right-click on the Zip drive's icon.
21. Click "Unmount".
22. The green triangle will go away.
23. It is now possible to take the Zip disk out of the drive.

Note

Hot-plugging the external USB Iomega Zip drive is not supported. This means you need to have the drive connected before you start Knoppix. You can't plug the Zip drive into the computer when it is already running and expect an icon for it to appear, as you can with USB flash drives and other USB external hard drives.

Using an internal IDE Iomega Zip drive

The internal IDE Iomega Zip disk drive is like an internal hard drive, but with removable writable media. Knoppix uses its built-in ATAPI (AT Attachment Packet Interface) driver to support the internal Iomega Zip drive. Typically the maximum disk capacity is 100 Mb. To copy files onto an internal Iomega Zip drive:

1. With the computer turned off, insert a PC formatted Zip disk into the Zip drive.
2. Start Knoppix in the usual way.
3. You will see an icon for the Zip drive on the Desktop. Assuming there are no other SCSI drives in your computer, the icon will belabelled "Hard disk partition [sda4]".
4. Click the icon for the Iomega Zip drive.
5. Wait for a moment while the Zip disk is mounted. A green triangle will appear indicating that the drive is in use.
6. Wait while the "Konqueror" file manager starts up.
7. The files on the disk will be displayed.

8. Right-click on the icon of the Zip drive.
9. Click "Change read/write mode".
10. Click "Yes".
11. Drag and drop the files you want to copy into the Zip drive window.
12. Click "Copy Here".
13. The files will be copied.
14. Close the Zip drive's windows.
15. Right click on the Zip drive icon.
16. Click "Unmount".
17. The green triangle will go away.
18. It is now safe to take the Zip disk out of the drive.

Using a parallel port Iomega Zip drive

The external parallel port Iomega Zip disk drive is the oldest kind of Zip drive. It was marketed for its high capacity, speed and portability. It is fully supported in Knoppix. Everything needed to use it is included in Knoppix, however, a "helping hand" is needed. To copy files onto an external parallel Zip drive:

1. With the computer turned off, connect the Zip drive to the computer's parallel (printer) port. Connect the Zip drive to the mains and turn the Zip drive on.
2. Insert a valid PC formatted Zip disk into the drive.
3. Start Knoppix, but at the boot prompt, specify text mode. For example, enter:

```
knoppix lang=uk 2
```

4. Knoppix will start up and then stop before loading KDE.
5. Press Enter on the keyboard to wake up the command prompt.
6. The next step is to enable the Iomega parallel Zip drive support. Look at the underside of the drive. The date of manufacture should be printed there. If your drive was made before 31 August 1998, enter this command and press Enter.

```
modprobe ppa
```

If your drive was made after 31 August 1998, type this and press Enter:

```
modprobe imm
```

7. If successful you will be rewarded with lines like this:

```
imm: Version 2.05 (for Linux 2.4.0)
imm: Found device at ID 6, Attempting to use EPP 16 bit
imm: Found device at ID 6, Attempting to use PS/2
imm: Communication established at 0x378 with ID 6 using PS/2
scsi3 : Iomega VPI2 (imm) interface
Vendor: IOMEGA Model: ZIP 250 Rev: K.47
```

```
Type: Direct-Access ANSI SCSI revision: 02
Attached scsi removable disk sda at scsi3, channel 0, id 6, lun 0
SCSI device sdb: 196608 512-byte hdwr sectors (101 MB)
sda: Write Protect is off
sda: sdb4
```

This means that the Linux kernel has found the Iomega external drive on the parallel port. In this example, the drive is called "sda", which means it is the first SCSI drive.

8. Type the following command and press Enter:

```
rebuildfstab -r -u knoppix -g knoppix
```

9. Finally type this and press Enter:

```
init 5
```

10. KDE will start up. You will see an icon for the Iomega Zip drive on the Desktop. Assuming you have no other SCSI drives, it will be labelled "Hard disk partition [sda4]".

11. Click the Zip drive icon.
12. Wait for a moment while the Zip drive is mounted.
13. Wait while the Konqueror file manager starts up.
14. The files on the Zip drive will be displayed.
15. Right-click on the Zip drive's icon.
16. Click "Change read/write mode".
17. Click "Yes".
18. Drag and drop the files and folders you wish to copy into the Zip drive's window.
19. Click "Copy Here".
20. The dropped items will be copied.
21. When you have finished copying, close the Zip drive's windows.
22. Right-click the Zip drive icon.
23. Click "Unmount".
24. The green triangle on the Zip drive icon will go away.
25. It is now safe to take the Zip disk out of the drive.

Using an Imation LS-120 SuperDisk

The Imation LS-120 SuperDisk drive crosses laser technology with the floppy disk. "LS" stands for "Laser Servo". Imation SuperDisk media has a capacity of 120 Mb. The Imation LS-120 SuperDisk was quite popular in the 1990s. For example, many computers made by Gateway came with a SuperDisk drive fitted as standard. Today, the SuperDisk drive is no longer made, but the 120 Mb media is still available.

The SuperDisk drive is an IDE device, like a CD-ROM drive. It does not use the conventional floppy drive interface. However, the SuperDisk drive is backwards compatible with 1.44 Mb floppy disk media.

Knoppix uses its built-in *AT Attachment Packet Interface* driver to support the Super-Disk drive. Knoppix uses SCSI emulation to treat the SuperDisk drive as a SCSI device. However, because of the way the drive works, it is not automatically detected so a little "helping hand" is needed. To copy files onto an Imation LS-120 SuperDisk drive:

1. Insert an LS-120 disk or conventional floppy disk into the SuperDisk drive.
2. Start Knoppix in the usual way.
3. Right-click anywhere on the Desktop.
4. Point to "Create New".
5. Click WHard Disk".
6. A window for the new device will appear.
7. On the "General" tab, replace the words "Hard Disk" with a suitable name. For example, enter "LS-120".
8. Click the „Device" tab.
9. In the "Device" drop-down box, choose /dev/sda, assuming there are no other SCSI devices in the system. Knoppix treats the SuperDisk drive as a SCSI device.
10. Click "OK".
11. The new device will appear on the Desktop.
12. Click the icon for the SuperDisk drive.
13. Wait while the device is mounted.
14. Wait while the Konqueror file manager starts up.
15. The files on the disk will be displayed.
16. Right-click on the icon of the LS-120 drive.
17. Click "Change read-write mode".
18. Click "Yes".
19. Drag and drop the files and folders you want to copy into the SuperDrive's window.
20. Click "Copy Here".
21. The items will be copied.
22. Close the SuperDisk's windows.
23. Right-click on the SuperDisk's icon.

24. Click "Unmount".
25. The green triangle on the drive's icon will go away.
26. It is now safe to take the disk out of the drive.

Quick help

Question: Why does it say "Do not format" on the LS-120 disk?

All LS-120 disks are factory formatted. Simply deleting all the files on the disk will put it back to factory fresh condition.

Connecting to a local areanetwork

Overview

Knoppix has built-in support for many Ethernet network cards. As a rule, if the computer has a network card, Knoppix will be able to support it (except the very old, or the very new). Well supported cards include 3Com, Realtek, NE2000 compatible, Intel and many others. However, some Broadcom cards, found in certain Dell PCs made after the year 2000, do not work with this version of Knoppix.

Automatic setup

If you have a supported network card, Knoppix will attempt to configure it automatically during startup. This is for you if you have a server which manages your local area network. To check to see if it worked:

1. Click the Konsole icon in the Panel (bottom row, 6th from the left).
2. Type this command and press Enter at the end of the line:
   ```
   ifconfig
   ```
3. You should see a response like this:

This says the first Ethernet interface (eth0) has been given the Internetworking Protocol (IP) address "192.168.1.18". If the Ethernet card has been given an IP address, it means the card is working. To double-check the connection, find out the IP address of another computer on your network. For example, suppose another computer has the address 192.168.1.1. Type this command and press Enter, replacing 192.168.1.1 appropriately:

```
ping 192.168.1.1
```

You should see a response like this:

Manual setup

If there is no server on your network, you will need to configure your network card manually.
1. Click the Knoppix menu in the bottom left corner.
2. Point to Network/Internet.
3. Click Network Card Configuration.
4. You will be asked if you want to use DHCP broadcast.
5. Click "No".
6. You will be asked to enter the IP address that you want to give to the first Ethernet interface. You need to know an IP address that is free on your network. You can't use an IP address that is already in use, or both computers will not be able to communicate.
7. Enter the IP address that you want to give to the card.
8. Click OK. Follow the prompts to complete the setup process.

Quick help

Question: There is no "eth0", why not?

Check the network cables. If there is a DHCP server on your local area network, make sure it is running. Click the "Knoppix" menu, choose "Root Shell" and enter:

```
/etc/init.d/network restart
pump -i eth0
```

Try configuring your network card manually. If it still won't work, it may mean your network card is not supported.

Using a network server

Knoppix can copy files to the following types of network file servers: File Transfer Protocol (FTP) servers. Windows Server Message Block (SMB) servers. UNIX Network File System (NFS) servers.

Copying to an FTP server

To copy files onto a File Transfer Protocol (FTP) server:
1.   Click the Konqueror icon in the Panel.
2.   The Konqueror file manager will come up.
3.   To log in to the FTP server anonymously, type the following on the address line. Replace '*server*' with the IP address of the server you want to connect to.
     ftp://server
     Example:
     ftp://192.168.1.1
4.   If you need a username and password to log in to the FTP server, type the following on the address line. Replace "username" and "password" with your username and password. Replace "server" with the address of the FTP server you want to connect to.
     ftp://username:password@server
     Example:
     ftp://phil:mypass@192.168.1.1
     This will connect to the FTP server at 192.168.1.1 with the username "phil" and password "mypass".
5.   The files on the FTP server will appear.
6.   Drag and drop the files you want to copy to that window.
7.   Click "Copy Here".
8.   The files will be uploaded, as long as you have permission to write files to the server.

Copying to a Windows file server

To copy files onto a Microsoft Windows file server:
1. Click the Konqueror icon in the Panel.
2. Wait while Konqueror starts up.
3. Type the following on the address line. Replace "server" with the hostname or IP address of the Windows file server.
    ```
    smb://server/
    ```
    Example:
    ```
    smb://192.168.1.1/
    ```
    The public shares on the server with the IP address 192.168.1.1 will be displayed. The workgroup name is detected automatically. If a username and password is required, replace "username" and "password" below with your username and password. Replace "server" with the IP address of the server you want to connect to.
    ```
    smb://username:password@server/
    ```
    Example:
    ```
    smb://phil:mypass@192.168.1.1/
    ```
    This will connect to the Windows file server at the IP address 192.168.1.1 with the username "phil" and password "mypass".
4. Drag and drop the files you want to copy into the server's Konqueror window.
5. Click "Copy Here".
6. The files will be copied, provided you have access permission to the Windows file server.

Copying to an NFS server

To copy files onto a Network File System (NFS) server:
1. Click the Knoppix menu in the bottom left corner.
2. Click "Root Shell".
3. Type the following command and press Enter:
    ```
    /etc/init.d/portmap start
    ```
4. The port mapping service will be started. The portmapper is needed to access NFS servers.
5. Enter the following command, again pressing Enter at the end of the line. Replace "server" with the IP address or hostname of your NFS server. Replace "/export" with the name of the shared directory on the NFS server.
    ```
    mount server:/export /home/knoppix/tmp
    ```
    For example, to mount the shared directory "/home" to the local directory "/home/knoppix/tmp":
    ```
    mount 192.168.1.1/home /home/knoppix/tmp
    ```
6. The NFS export should be mounted.
7. Click the "Home" icon in the Panel.
8. The files in the Knoppix home directory will be displayed.
9. Click the "tmp" folder.

10. The shared directory on the NFS server should appear.
11. Drag and drop the files you wish to copy into this window.
12. Click "Copy Here".
13. Given that you have the appropriate file permissions on the NFS server, the files will be copied.

Connecting to the Internet

The main ways to get connected to the Internet are:

Through an Ethernet gateway, router or local area network.

Through an external serial modem.

Through a PCMCIA serial cardbus modem.

Knoppix is designed first and foremost for wired Ethernet networking. This gives you the best chance of success. Meanwhile, the following connection methods may not be so easy with Knoppix:

Most internal PCI dial-up modems.

Most external USB broadband modems.

Most wireless (802.11) PCI and PCMCIA cards.

Some PCMCIA modem/network combination cards.

AOL and Compuserve.

The above methods tend to rely on proprietary software that requires Microsoft Windows. Even if the proprietary software were available for Linux (which it sometimes is these days) it cannot be distributed with Knoppix due to licence constraints.

Broadband

A *broadband* Internet connection lets you download at up to ten times the speed of a conventional modem. It also lets you make and receive voice calls on the same line at the same time. The technical name is *Asynchronous Digital Subscriber Line* (ADSL). To use ADSL broadband Internet over a conventional phone line with Knoppix, you need:

A telephone line which has been "activated" for ADSL.

An account with a ADSL-enabled Internet Service Provider. This means any ISP that offers a standard broadband service.

A microfilter for each standard analogue device (such as telephones, fax machines, and dialup modems).

A supported Ethernet adapter in your PC or laptop (see the section "Connecting to a local area network").

An ADSL router. These popular, inexpensive devices combine a broadband modem with an Ethernet router and gateway, giving "instant Internet". The single-port variety is for one computer.

Multi-port versions let several computers share the same broadband Internet connection.

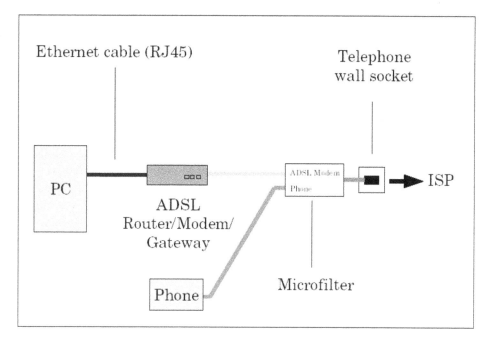

To make the connection:

1. Make sure the Ethernet cable from the ADSL router is connected to the computer's Ethernet adapter.
2. Start Knoppix. It should detect the network card and then obtain an IP address automatically from the ADSL router.
3. If you have not already done so, use a web browser to visit the ADSL router's configuration page. To learn about the web browsers included in Knoppix, see the later section, "Browsing the World Wide Web". Enter the necessary information on the configuration page to make the connection to your ISP.
4. You're done! As long as the "upstream" connection to the Internet is working, you will be connected to the Internet.

Note

The diagram above shows a typical setup for the UK. It may vary from country to country depending on regulatory requirements. What is most important is that filtering must be done correctly. The ADSL modem must never be subject to filtering, while every other device on the telephone line must be filtered. The term "broadband" can also mean Internet provided by cable and other high speed Internet connections (including wireless options). These connections may or may not be usable in Knoppix.

Dial-up

Dial-up Internet is the older, slower way to access the Internet. To connect this way, you need an account with any standard Internet Service Provider (not AOL or Compuserve) and one of the following:

An external serial modem. This type of modem connects to the computer's serial port (called COM1 or COM2 under DOS). No special driver is needed to operate this type of modem, so compatibility with Knoppix is excellent. For example, the "Sitecom External V92 Serial Modem" works perfectly.

A PCMCIA Cardbus modem. A PCMCIA Cardbus modem is effectively an external serial modem. In general, the cheaper the card, the better. For example, the "Sitecom 56Kbps Fax Modem PC Card" works perfectly with Knoppix.

An internal ISA modem. Like the external modem, this type of modem needs no special driver to make it work. That is why old ISA modems are useful.

There are two main ways to make a dial-up connection. The recommended way is to use "K Point to Point Protocol" (KPPP). The alternative, in case KPPP doesn't work, is the "Worldvisions Dialer" (WVDial).

Connecting using KPPP

1. Click the Knoppix menu in the lower left corner.
2. Point to "Network/Internet".
3. Click "Modem Dialer".

4. The "KDE Point-To-Point Protocol" (KPPP) program will start.

5. Click "Setup".
6. Click the "Device" tab.

7. If your modem is plugged into the serial port called "COM1" in Windows, set "Modem device" to /dev/ttyS0. If it is plugged into the port called "COM2" in Windows, select /dev/ttyS1. If you have a PCMCIA Card-bus modem, select /dev/modem. If you have an internal ISA modem, select /dev/ttyS0 first; if that doesn't work, try up to /dev/ttyS3.

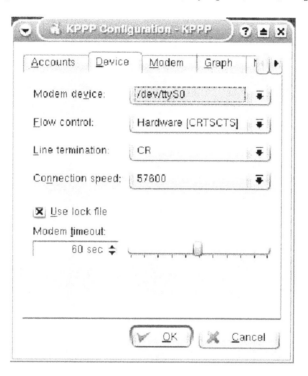

8. Click the "Modem" tab.
9. Click "Query modem".
10. You should see a response from the modem. If not, go back to step 7 and try another modem device setting.

11. Click the "Accounts" tab.

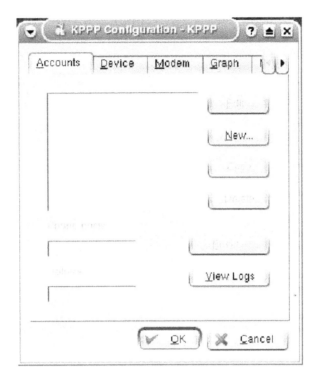

12. Click "New".
13. Click "Dialog setup".

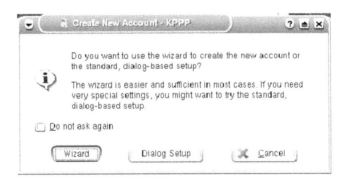

14. In "Connection name" enter a name for the connection eg "test".
15. Beside "Phone number", click "Add".
16. Enter your Internet Service Provider's dial-up access number. If you don't
    know, ask your Internet Service Provider. Click OK.

17. Click OK. This will take you back to the accounts screen.
18. Click OK again.
19. Enter your login ID and password. Again, if you don't know what they are, ask your Internet Service Provider.

20. Click Connect.
21. You should hear the modem work.
22. In a few moments, the KPPP window should shrink down to the Taskbar. It should then read "00:00" on the Taskbar. This indicates your time online in hours and minutes. Congratulations, you have connected to the Internet successfully.

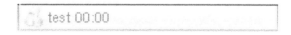

23. To disconnect, click the KPPP button in the Taskbar.
24. The KPPP window will come back up.
25. Click Disconnect.
26. The phone call will be ended.

Quick help

Question: It says "The PPP daemon died unexpectedly!"
Check your username and password.

Question: I know my username and password is correct but it still says "The PPP daemon died unexpectedly".
Try another modem.

Question: I tried another modem and I still can't connect.
Sorry, it seems that KPPP doesn't work with all ISPs. Luckily, there is an alternative. The "Worldvisions Dialer" is included with Knoppix. For an example of how to use "wvdial", see:

```
http://support.real-time.com/linux/dialup/wvdial.html
```

Question: Can I use an internal PCI modem?
Not usually. As noted in the "Identifying hardware" section, most internal PCI modem cards need special software not in Knoppix.

Question: I have a PCMCIA combo Ethernet modem card, but the modem function doesn't work.
Sorry, with some combo Ethernet and modem PCMCIA cards, only one part works. Usually the Ethernet works and the modem does not.

Browsing the Web

Once you have an Internet connection, Knoppix has several different *browsers* built in. A browser is a program for using the World Wide Web, one of the Internet's most popular services.

For a quick start, click Konqueror Web Browser on the Panel.
For a more sophisticated web browser, click the "Mozilla Browser" button on the Panel. Mozilla Web Browser takes longer to start than Konqueror, especially on slower computers with limited RAM.
For a minimal web browser, click K menu -> Internet -> Dillo.
For text-only web browsing (yes, really), click K menu -> Internet -> Lynx. Then hit the letter G (for Go). You will be prompted to enter the web address that you want to visit. Type the web address that you want, then press Enter. The web page will be loaded.

Email

Knoppix has several different *email clients*. An email client is a program that lets you send and receive Internet email. Here is how to set up the KMail email client in Knoppix:

1. Click the K menu in the bottom left corner.
2. Point to "Internet".
3. Click "KMail (Mail Client)".

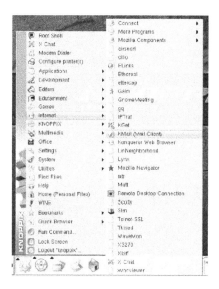

4. The KMail mail program will be loaded.

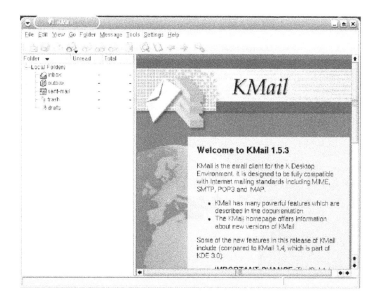

5. Click the "Settings" menu.
6. Click "Configure KMail".
7. The KMail configuration screen will appear. On the left side, ensure that "Identities" is selected. Click "Modify".
8. Enter your real name, organisation and email address, then click OK.

9. Click "Network"
10. Click "Remove".

11. In the "Host" box, enter the hostname of your Internet Service Provider's outgoing SMTP (Simple Mail Transfer Protocol) server. If the SMTP server requires authentication, check the "Server requires authentication" box and enter your username and password for sending mail.

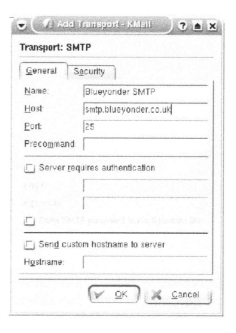

12. Click OK.
13. Click the "Receiving" tab.
14. Click "Add".
15. Select the type of incoming mail server you have. Most Internet Service Providers use POP (Post Office Protocol). Some provide *IMAP* (Internet Message Application Protocol).
16. Click OK.
17. In the "Name" box, enter a description for this email account. In "Login", enter your username for receiving email. In "Password", enter your password for receiving email. In "Host", enter your Internet Service Provider's incoming mail server address.
18. Uncheck "Delete message from server after fetching". This preserves the messages in your incoming mailbox so that you can still receive them using another email program later. (see page 70)
19. Click OK, then OK again.
20. To see if you have new mail, click the "File" menu, then "Check Mail". Or click the "Check Mail In" button on the Toolbar.
21. To write email, click the "Message" menu, then "New Message". Or click the "New Message" button on the Toolbar. When you have finished writing, click the "Message" menu, then "Send", or click the "Send" button in the Toolbar.

Important

Knoppix will not let you accidentally run programs received by email. Program files must be given *execute permission* before they can be run by double-clicking on them. This gives excellent protection against would-be "email viruses", while still letting you open ordinary document attachments easily.

Printing

Knoppix has built-in support for hundreds of popular printers. Parallel and USB connections are supported. The best supported inkjet printers are HP and Epson. Many Canon and a few Lexmark printers are also supported. On the laser front, greyscale Postscript and most greyscale Printer Control Language (PCL) laser printers work.

However, some printers do not work with Knoppix. The printers that do not work tend to be cheap Lexmark inkjet printers and very low cost colour laser printers. Colour laser printers work if they are fully Postscript or PCL compatible. Unfortunately, low cost colour laser printers tend to support neither Postscript nor PCL and may therefore be completely incompatible with Knoppix.

Web link
The Linux printing home page:
http://www.linuxprinting.org/

To set up a printer connected by a USB or a parallel cable:
1. Click the Knoppix icon in the Panel.
2. Point to "Configure".
3. Click "Configure printer(s)".

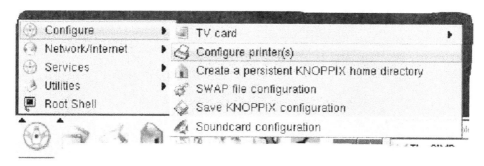

4. Wait for a moment while the KDE "Printing Manager" starts.

5. Click "Add".
6. Click "Add Printer/Class...".
7. The welcome screen of the "Add Printer" wizard will appear.
8. Click Next.

9. Select "Local printer", then click Next.

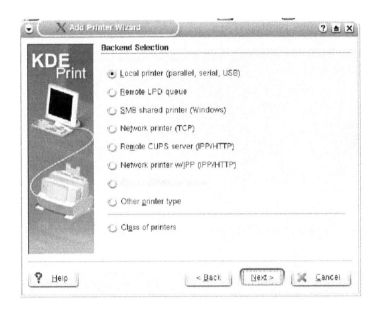

10. Select the port that your printer is on. If your printer is connected to the computer's parallel port, select Parallel Port #1 (/dev/lp0). If you have a USB printer, select USB Printer #1 (/dev/usb/lp0). Click Next.

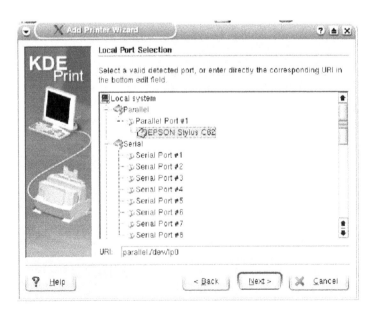

11. Select the manufacturer and model of your printer. If you cannot find your exact printer model in the list, see Quick Help below. Click Next.

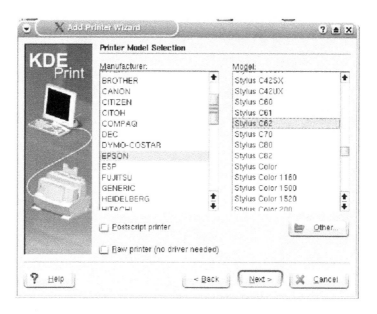

12. This screen appears if Knoppix knows of more than one driver that can operate your printer. Usually the first or the recommended option will be fine. Click Next.

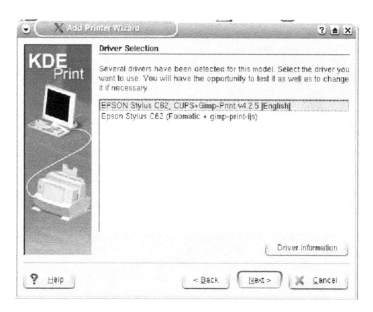

13. Click the "Test" button to print a test page on your printer. After a short pause, your printer should start working. If not, see the Quick Help section below.

14. When the test page has finished, click Next four times until you get to the "General Information" screen. Enter a short name for your printer, then click Next.

15. Click Finish to return to the Printing Manager.

16. When you exit Knoppix, the printer setup will be lost. However, there is a way to save it for next time. See the later section, "Finding permanence".

Quick help

Question: What should I do if my printer isn't in the list?

Look up your printer on `www.linuxprinting.org`. It may tell you which driver that is in the list will work with your printer. For example, the generic "HP Deskjet" driver produces basic printing results on most of the HP Deskjet series of printers. A newer version of Knoppix will contain a more up-to-date printer listing. The web site may tell you that your printer is not supported at all by Free Software (sorry). If you still want to print using Knoppix, see the "Recommended printers" section of the web site for buying advice.

Question: Why does the test page leave a gap at the bottom?

The test page paper size is US Letter by default. If you are using A4 paper, the test page won't print all the way to the bottom of the page. This is normal.

Question: I have an Epson printer. It is detected in the Add Printer wizard and the connection looks good. When I send a test page to the printer, it says "Test page successfully sent to printer" but then nothing happens. No lights flash on the printer and there is no error on the computer. What is wrong?

Some Epson printers need to be put into "Packet Mode" (by printing a nozzle check page) before they will work with Linux. Until then, some Epson printers will not respond to any commands. To solve the problem:

1. Click the Knoppix menu.
2. Click "Root Shell".
3. Make sure your Internet connection is working, then using Root Shell, run the following commands, assuming the Epson printer is connected via USB and it is the first USB printer:

```
wget www.pjls16812.pwp.blueyonder.co.uk/knowingknoppix/epsonfix.tar.gz
tar xvzf epsonfix.tar.gz
cat nozzlecmd.raw > /dev/usb/lp0
```

If the printer is connected via a parallel cable, substitute:
```
cat nozzlecmd.raw > /dev/lp0
```

The printer should wake up and print the nozzle check page. If it doesn't respond, turn the printer off and on, then try again. The printer should then work normally in both Linux and Windows. The normal Linux command for printing an Epson nozzle check is called `escputil`. Unfortunately, `escputil` is not included in Knoppix version 3.3. To get around the problem, we have put a copy of the raw data for an Epson printer nozzle check on the Knowing Knoppix website.

Scanning

Knoppix has built-in support for some scanners. Scanning in Knoppix is simple, if you are lucky enough to have a fully compatible scanner. Scanner support is provided by a program called "Scanner Access Is Now Easy". If your scanner is fully supported, you don't have to do any setup at all. To test a scanner using Knoppix:

1. Click K menu.
2. Click Multimedia.
3. Click XScanImage.
4. If the scanner is detected, the device name will be shown at the top of the window. For example, if you have an Epson Perfection 1260 USB, it will say `Plustek:/dev/usbscanner`.
5. Assuming your scanner is detected, click "Preview Window".
6. Click Acquire Preview.
7. The image that the scanner sees will be shown.
8. Lasoo the area to be scanned using the mouse.
9. Click "Scan".
10. The marked area will be scanned to an image file.

Web link
The Scanner Access Is Now Easy home page:
http://www.sane-project.org/

Sound

Knoppix has built-in support for many sound cards. Well supported cards include Soundblaster compatibles, Creative Soundblaster Live, CMedia 8738, Intel i810, Ensoniq, Crystal Soundfusion and the Via 82c series of sound cards.

Testing sound in KDE

1. Click K Menu.
2. Point to Settings.
3. Click Control Center. (see figure on next page)
4. Wait for a moment while the "KDE Control Center" starts.
5. On the left side, click Sound & Multimedia.
6. Under Sound & Multimedia, click Sound System.
7. On the right side, click "Start aRTs server on KDE startup".

8. Click Apply.
9. Click Test Sound.
10. You should hear the KDE startup sound.

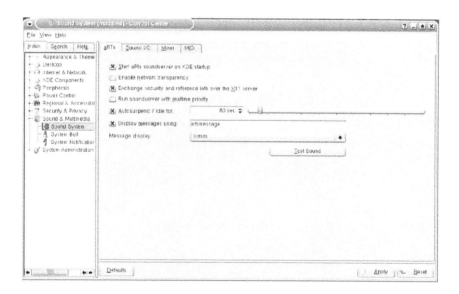

Testing sound in XMMS

To play the built-in demonstration music file:
1. Click the CD-ROM icon for your Knoppix CD.
2. Click the "Demos" folder.
3. Click the "Audio" folder.
4. Click the "opensource.ogg" file.

5. Wait while the "X Multimedia System" application starts.
6. The demonstration song will play.

If the demonstration song does not start automatically, click the "Play" button (bottom row, second from the left, in the XMMS window).

Volume controls

To adjust the sound volume levels:
1. Click K Menu -> Multimedia -> Sound -> KMix (Sound Mixer).
2. The main volume control is on the far left. Move the slider up for louder and down for quieter.

To learn what each slider does, hover the mouse pointer over the icon at the top. A little yellow label will appear, such as "Microphone".

Muting

The green spots are called the "mute buttons". The mute button turns on and off output from the corresponding channel. Light green means on, dark means off (muted). All the channels are on by default.

> **Note**
> The microphone channel has no output, since it's only used for recording (input). KMix gives the microphone channel a mute button anyway. The mute button on the microphone channel has no effect.

Closing KMix

When you close KMix, it goes into the System Tray which is in the bottom right corner of the screen. To get KMix back again, right-click its icon in the System Tray, then click "Show Mixer Window".

Quick help

Question: I can't get KMix to start by clicking in the K menu.
KMix is already started. Right-click its icon in the System Tray (bottom right corner of the screen), then click "Show Mixer Window".

Sound recording

This explains how to test sound recording through your sound card. You need a microphone plugged in to the "Mic" socket on your sound card.

1. Bring up the KMix window. If KMix is already running, right-click its icon in the System Tray, then click "Show Mixer Window". If KMix is not already running, click K Menu -> Multimedia ->Sound -> KMix (Sound Mixer).
2. Click the red button at the bottom of the Microphone channel. This sets KMix to record from the Microphone channel. You can only record from one channel at a time.

3. Click K menu -> Multimedia -> Sound -> Audacity.
4. Wait for a moment while the "Audacity" application starts up.
5. To start recording, click the large red circle (record) button.

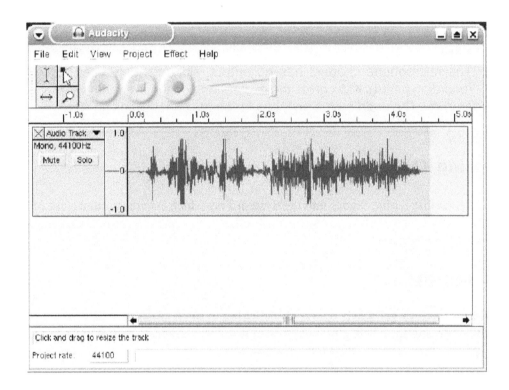

Audacity is a multi-track sound recorder. Each new recording that you make is stored in a new track. This lets you overlay sounds on top of each other. To get rid of a recorded track, click the small X on the left side next to the words "Audio Track".

Web links

X Multimedia System:
http://www.xmms.org/
Audacity sound recorder:
http://audacity.sourceforge.net/

Playing audio CDs

Knoppix has a built-in player for *Compact Disc Digital Audio* music CDs. Unlike data CDs, audio CDs don't need to be mounted in order to be played. The ideal is to have two CD drives in your computer ñ one for the Knoppix CD, and one for the audio CD that you want to play. If you only have one CD drive, refer to "If you have only one CD drive" in the "Advanced startup options" section.

1. Click K Menu.
2. Point to Multimedia.
3. Point to Sound.
4. Click KsCD (CD Player).
5. The CD player application will appear.
6. Put the audio CD in the drive that is not occupied by Knoppix.
7. Click the big "Play" button in the KsCD window to begin.

8. The audio CD will be played.

If your CD-ROM drive is wired to the sound card, you will hear the music through the speakers attached to the sound card. If you can't hear anything, plug your speakers or headphones into the audio out socket on the front of the CD drive. Then adjust the volume level using the volume control on the front of the CD drive.

When you close KsCD, it will "dock" into the System Tray in the bottom right corner of the screen. To get it back again, click its icon in the System Tray.

> **Note**
> Some audio CDs are designed not to work on a computer CD-ROM drive. They should be clearly marked. They may also not work on some non-computer CD players such as in-car players. If you are not satisfied with your audio CD, return it to the shop and ask for a refund. It is simply cheaper and easier for the seller to give you your money back than argue.

Playing DVD movies

Knoppix has a built-in player for DVD movies. This section will help you test a DVD-ROM drive for DVD movie playing. It is best to have two CD drives - one CD drive for the Knoppix disc, and one DVD capable drive for the movie disc you want to play. If you have just a single DVD drive, refer to "If you have only one CD drive" in the "Advanced startup options" section.

What is DVD?

DVD stands for *Digital Versatile Disc*. It was originally called *Digital Video Disc*. A DVD disc can contain data, audio or video. DVD Read Only Memory (ROM) drives are backwards compatible with CD-ROM drives, so they can read Compact Disc media.

DVD movies in Knoppix

Unfortunately, Knoppix cannot play most commercial DVD movie discs. It can only play DVD movie discs that are *unencrypted*. Even more unfortunately, there is no label to tell you which discs are encrypted and which are not. The DVDs that are most likely to work are:

Home-made, demonstration or movie trailer discs.

Discs without a *DVD Region* label. Technically, these are called "Any Region" discs.

A region code attempts to stop a disc sold in one country working in another country. A disc with a region code is marked with a world globe containing a number between 1 and 8. The suggested media for testing purposes is a demo or movie trailer disc without a region code. For example, "Movie Trailers" DVDs are both unencrypted and all-region.

Playing

It is best to have two CD drives: one drive for Knoppix, and one DVD capable drive for the movie disc. To play an unencrypted DVD movie:

1. Click K Menu.
2. Point to Multimedia.
3. Point to Video.
4. Click Xine Media Player.
5. Wait for a moment while "Xine" starts up.
6. The Xine player application will appear.
7. Put the disc in the DVD drive that is not occupied by Knoppix.

8.   Click the "DVD" button in Xine.

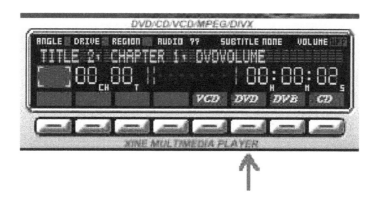

9.   If the DVD is unencrypted, and the region check is passed, the movie should begin playing.

10. If it says "Error reading NAV packet", most likely this means the DVD is encrypted and so it cannot be played. Try another disc.

Changing the region

Some discs have a DVD Region code but are not encrypted. These are rare. Xine uses "Region 1 (US / Canada / US Territories)" by default.

DVD Region Codes
1: U.S., Canada, U.S. Territories
2: Japan, Europe, South Africa, and Middle East (including Egypt)
3: Southeast Asia and East Asia (including Hong Kong)
4: Australia, New Zealand, Pacific Islands, Central America, Mexico, South America, and the Caribbean
5: Eastern Europe (Former Soviet Union), Indian subcontinent, Africa, North Korea, and Mongolia
6: China
7: Reserved
8: Special international venues (airplanes, cruise ships, etc.)

To change the region:

1. Click the Xine Setup button. When you hover the mouse pointer over the "Setup" button, a blue spanner icon will appear in the Xine display, and a "Setup window" tooltip will appear.

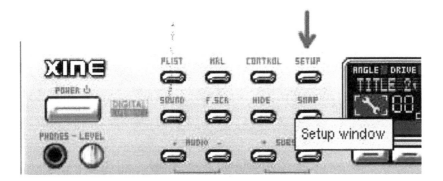

2. Click the "Input" tab.
3. Under "Region that DVD player claims to be", choose the region number that you want. For example, choose "2" for United Kingdom (Europe).

4. Click Apply, then Close.

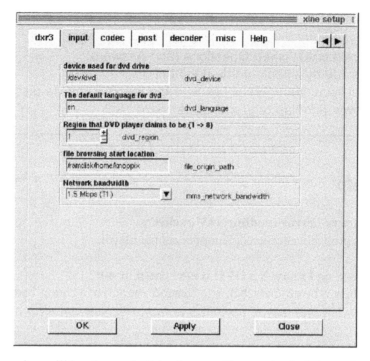

5. The region will be changed. This change affects only the Xine software. It will not alter your DVD drive. It will not affect any other DVD movie playing software that you may have.

Why don't encrypted DVDs work?

Encrypted DVDs do not work with Knoppix because "Xine Media Player" has not been authorised by the "DVD Copy Control Association". Getting authorisation is expensive and highly restrictive. An authorised DVD playing application cannot be distributed with Knoppix, because of licence constraints. Therefore, Knoppix only has limited support for DVD movies.

Content Scrambling System

DVD encryption works using "Content Scrambling System" (CSS). It is described as "copy control", but it actually only affects playback.

DeCSS

Of course, for every wall there is a higher ladder. An (in)famous person called "DVD Jon" discovered how to make a fully functional yet unauthorised DVD movie player. The result is called "DeCSS". DeCSS allows commercial DVD playing in Xine. However, DeCSS cannot be distributed with Knoppix, for legal reasons.

> **Web links**
> Xine Media Player
> http://xinehq.de/
> DVD Frequently Asked Questions (and Answers)
> http://dvddemystified.com/dvdfaq.html
> A partial list of commercial but Xine friendly DVD movie discs:
> http://www.videolan.org/removed/freedvd.html

Quick help

Question: It says "Error reading NAV packet".
The movie is probably encrypted. Knoppix cannot play it.

Question: How do I know if a DVD is encrypted or not?
You don't. There is no official label. The presence (or not) of a region code is a guide but not definitive. The only way to find out is to try it with Xine and see if it works.

Other applications

Knoppix includes many other useful and fun applications. There isn't space to describe them all fully here. In this section are some of the highlights to look out for.

Graphics

The Gimp

The GNU Image Manipulation Program (The Gimp) is a wonderful graphics editor. It is for painting, image editing and photo retouching. Many people think The Gimp is the greatest thing after Linux itself. To start using it:

click K menu -> Multimedia -> Graphics -> The Gimp.

The screenshot below shows Wilber, the Gimp's mascot. Wilber was created by Tuomas Kuosmanen, also known as "Tiger T". Underneath is the Gimp Toolbox, and a Brushes dialog.

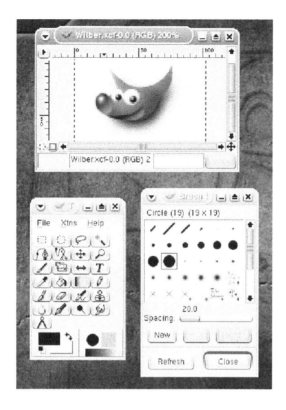

Office applications

OpenOffice.org office suite
OpenOffice.org is the slowest but most powerful office application in Knoppix. Open-Office.org combines word processing, spreadsheets, presentations and drawing in one huge package. On older computers, OpenOffice.org may take several minutes to start. To begin using OpenOffice.org, click K menu -> Office -> OpenOffice.org -> OpenOffice.

KOffice
KOffice is a simple office suite, for word-processing, spreadsheet, drawing, presentations and other tasks. Unlike OpenOffice, KOffice is quick to start. To begin, click K menu -> Office -> KOffice, then click the program you would like to use.

Gnumeric
Gnumeric is a powerful standalone spreadsheet application. Like KOffice, Gnumeric is quick to start. To begin, click K menu -> Office -> Gnumeric.

AbiWord
AbiWord is a simple word standalone processor. To get started, click K menu -> Office -> AbiWord word processor.

Toys and amusements

KStars planetarium

KStars shows the position of the stars and planets in the sky in real time. KStars can show the view of the sky from hundreds of locations around the world. It also has a catalogue of planets, stars and other objects. To start using KStars, click K menu -> Entertainment -> Science -> KStars.

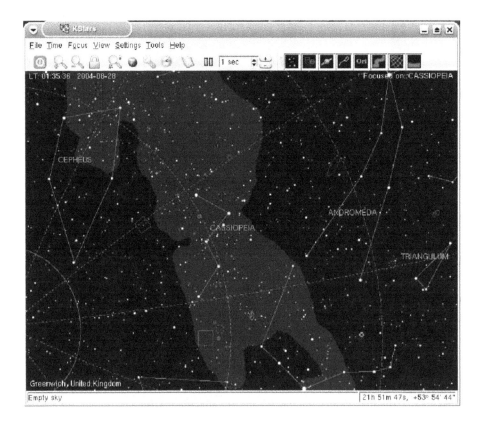

Frozen Bubble

Frozen Bubble is an arcade style bubble bursting game for one or two players. The idea is to hit two or more other bubbles of the same colour to make them disappear. To start, click K menu -> Games -> Tetris-like -> Frozen-Bubble.

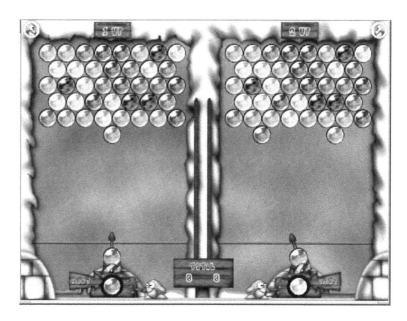

KSokoban

KSokoban is a gemstone-pushing puzzle game. The object of the game is to move the red diamonds onto the green circles, only by pushing the red diamonds. Move the man using the cursor keys. To begin, click K menu -> Games -> Tactics & Strategy -> KSokoban.

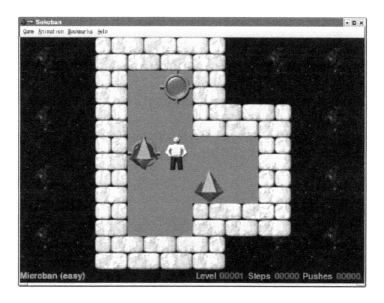

GTans

GTans is a shape-building puzzle game. Move, rotate and flip the shapes to make the larger shape shown on the right hand side. To start, click K menu -> Games -> Puzzles -> GTans.

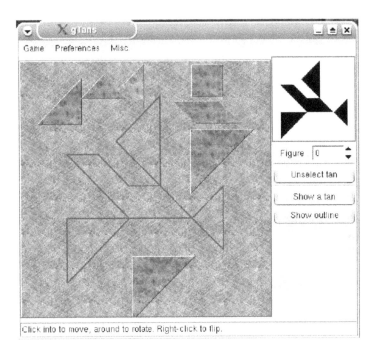

Recovering from freezes

It is possible for the X Window System, the K Desktop Environment, or an individual application to "freeze up". This section explains what to do if that happens.

Getting rid of an individual application

The most common situation is to have a program that just doesn't seem to want to go away. Even when you click the close button on its window, it still won't disappear. To get rid of it:

1. Press Ctrl+Alt+Esc on the keyboard.
2. The pointer will change into a skull and crossbones.
3. Point anywhere inside the window that you want to get rid of.
4. Click the left mouse button.
5. The errant program will be killed.

Restarting the X Window System

If more than one program seems to be stuck, you may need to restart the X Window System. To do that:

1. Press Ctrl+Alt+F2.
2. Type this command, then press Enter:
   ```
   init 2
   ```
3. You will see the message "X Window System shut down". This will also end the K Desktop Environment and all its open applications.
4. Then enter:
   ```
   init 5
   ```
5. The X Window System will be restarted. The KDE desktop will appear again as it did when you first started Knoppix.

Getting help

"Where's the 'Any' key?" — Homer Simpson

How to get help

On the CD

The Knoppix CD carries the official list of frequently asked questions and answers. It is provided in several languages. To read the English version:

1. Click the CD-ROM icon for your Knoppix CD
2. Click the "KNOPPIX" folder.
3. Click the "KNOPPIX-FAQ-EN.txt" file.
4. Wait for a moment while the "KWrite" application starts.
5. The English version of the "Frequently Asked Questions" file will appear.

From the Web

See the "unofficial" Knoppix web site for further FAQs, user forums, and how to get the latest version of Knoppix.

Web link
The site for users, developers, and testers of Knoppix
http://www.knoppix.net/

By email

There is a mailing list, which is for development of Knoppix. The discussions are in German and English.

The mailing list homepage is:
http://mailman.linuxtag.org/mailman/listinfo/debian-knoppix

The archives are at:

http://mailman.linuxtag.org/pipermail/debian-knoppix/

With Internet Relay Chat

If you are looking for somewhat instant answers, Internet Relay Chat (IRC) is the place to be. To talk to other Knoppix users using IRC:

1. Make sure you are connected to the Internet.
2. Click K Menu.
3. Point to Internet.
4. Click X Chat.
5. Wait for a moment while the "X Chat" application starts.
6. In the Nick Names boxes, enter up to three nicknames which you would like to be known as. You must enter at least two nicknames, in case your preferred nickname happens to be in use when you join the chat server.
7. In the Username box, enter the username or login which you use to connect to your Internet Service Provider.
8. In the Real Name box, type your real name.
9. Under "Networks", scroll down to "Freenode".
10. Click "FreeNode".

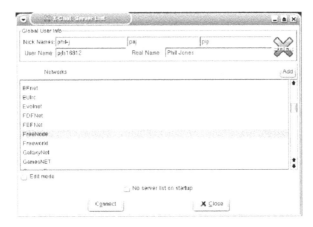

11. Click "Connect".

12. The message of the day from the IRC server will be shown.
13. Type the following command and press Enter:

/join #knoppix

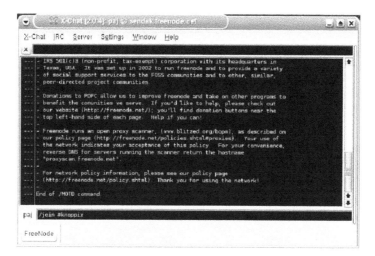

14. You will be joined to the "#knoppix" IRC channel. The messages in the channel will appear on the left. The nicknames of the people who are in the channel will be shown on the right.
15. Ask your question, remembering to spell and punctuate correctly. The other IRC users will do their best to help you. Enjoy the chat!

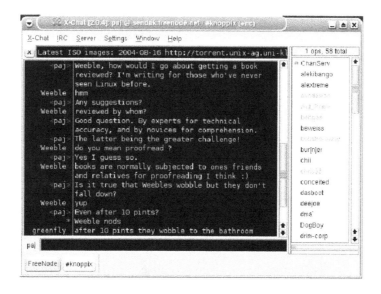

Tip

Before using IRC, check to see if your question is already answered in the Frequently Asked Questions. Knoppix users would love to see more people using IRC. However, if you ask a question that is already answered in the Frequently Asked Questions, you may be told to look there - or maybe something ruder!

Making X Chat fonts larger

If you find the writing too small in X Chat:

1. Click the "Settings" menu at the top of the X Chat window.
2. Click "Preferences".
3. Next to "Font", click "Browse".
4. Choose the font size you would like to use.

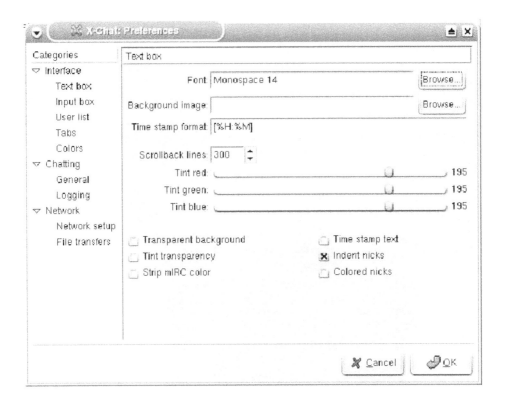

5. Click OK.
6. Click OK.
7. The fonts will change to the size you chose.

Finding permanence

"The box said that I needed to have Windows 98 or better... so I installed Linux." — *LinuxNewbie.org*

Overview

Knoppix lets you store personalised settings, document files and system settings on a disk. This saves you from having to set up Knoppix from scratch every time you run it.

Creating a persistent Home directory

Personalisation is what makes your computer yours. Personalised settings include application preferences, for example, your favourite KDE background wallpaper. Documents are the files that you create using Knoppix applications, such as graphics and word processed document files. Personalised settings and documents are stored in a special place called your *Home directory*.

Knoppix lets you keep your Home directory on another disk. This is called creating a *persistent Knoppix home directory*. It allows you to use a personalised Knoppix account everywhere you go. For example, this allows you to sit down at one computer, do some work, move to another computer and carry on working.

This works best with a USB hard drive stick, also known as a USB flash drive. It gives you hundreds of megabytes of storage in a space no bigger than a key fob. A USB flash drive is an ideal companion for Knoppix.

To create a persistent Home directory on a USB flash drive:

1. Insert your USB flash drive.
2. Wait for a moment while the drive is detected.
3. A new hard disk partition icon will appear on the Desktop.
4. Note the name of the new icon. For example, if there are no other SCSI drives in the computer, it will be labelled "Hard disk partition [sda1]".
5. Right-click on the USB flash drive icon.
6. Click "Mount".
7. Right-click on the USB flash drive icon again.
8. Click "Change read/write mode".
9. It will ask if you want to make the partition writable.
10. Click "Yes".
11. Click the Knoppix menu in the Panel.
12. Point to "Configure".

13. Click "Create persistent KNOPPIX home directory".

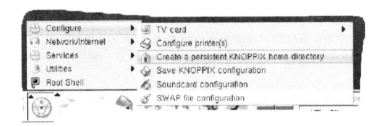

14. Click "Yes".

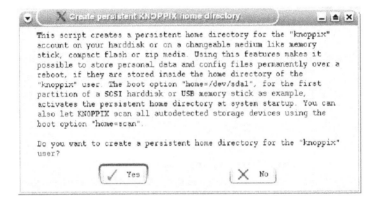

15. Choose the partition that corresponds to your flash drive. In this example, /dev/sda1 represents the flash drive.

16. You will be asked if you want to encrypt the file that will be created on the flash drive. This is optional, so click "No".

17. Enter how big in megabytes you would like your Knoppix home directory to be. For example, enter ì100î for 100 megabytes. Imagine you have a 256 Mb

flash drive. This will create a 100 megabyte file on the flash drive, leaving 156 Mb free for other files.

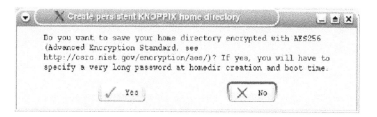

18. Click OK.
19. Wait while Knoppix prepares the flash drive. If the flash drive has an activity light, you will see it working for a few moments.
20. You will be asked if you want to use the entire partition. Click "No". This will leave existing files on the flash drive alone.

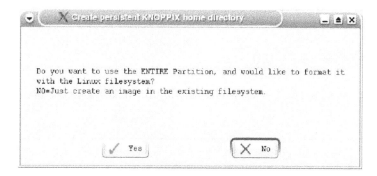

21. Wait while Knoppix completes the setup process.

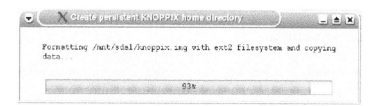

22. Knoppix will tell you what you need to type at the boot prompt to use the persistent Knoppix home directory on your flash drive. Make a note of what it says, then click OK.

Knowing Knoppix

You must reboot for the change to take effect. Shut down Knoppix and restart. At the boot prompt, type the following command, replacing "sda1" as appropriate:

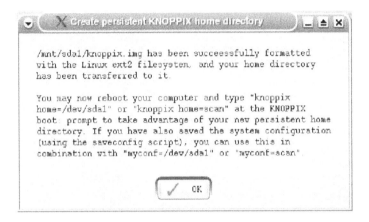

```
knoppix home=/mnt/sda1
```

During startup you should see a message like this:

```
Mounting /mnt/sda1/knoppix.img as /home/knoppix...
/home/knoppix mounted OK.
```

This means it worked. The USB flash drive will now be used for the home directory of the "knoppix" user.

Important

With a persistent home directory on a flash drive, the flash drive will be in use all the time. Do not take the flash drive out until you have shut down Knoppix.

Saving system settings

Saving system settings is called making a *Knoppix configuration archive*. This stores settings that are saved in the system-wide configuration directory, not in the home directory. For example, it allows you to save your printer setup, so you don't have to do it again next time. To save the system settings:

1. Click the Knoppix menu on the Panel.
2. Point to "Configure".
3. Click "Save KNOPPIX configuration".

4. Select the system settings that you would like to store.

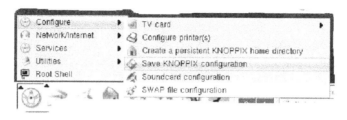

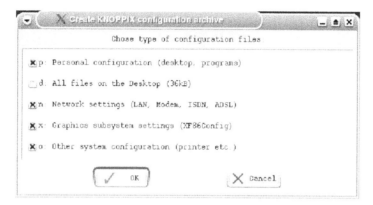

Personal configuration. If you have a persistent Knoppix home directory, you do not need this. If you do not have a persistent Knoppix home directory, this option covers the personalised settings you have made in programs like the KDE Control Center, and your personalised settings in applications such as AbiWord. It does not include document files, such as saved word processor files. It also does not include cache files from web browsing.

All files on the Desktop. If you have a persistent Knoppix home directory, you do not need this. If you do not have a persistent Knoppix home directory, select this option to save the new disk icons or program icons that you may have created on the Desktop.

Network settings. If you have a persistent Knoppix home directory, and all you are doing is using the KPPP dialler to connect to the Internet via a modem, you do not need this. KPPP configuration is saved as part of your Knoppix home directory. The network settings saved by this option include Local Area Network (LAN), manually configured dial-up networking (modem), Integrated Services Digital Network (ISDN) and Asynchronous Digital Subscriber Line (ADSL) settings. For example, if you have set up your network card manually, select this option to save the configuration for next time.

Graphics subsystem settings. This saves settings for the "X Window System" (the graphics display). For example, if you specified a certain screen resolution when you started Knoppix, this option will save that setting.

Other system configuration. This option saves the printer setup and all other system-wide settings.

5. Click OK.
6. Select the device that you would like to save onto. For example, assuming you have a USB flash drive, and there are no other SCSI drives in the system, choose /mnt/sda1.

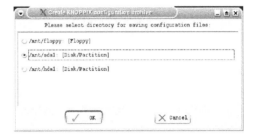

7. Click OK.
8. Wait while the archive is created.

9. If it worked, it will say, "Creation of the KNOPPIX configuration archive was successful". It will tell you the command to use at the boot prompt to load the saved settings.

10. Click OK to exit.

To load the saved settings next time you start Knoppix, use the "myconfig" parameter at the boot prompt. For example, assuming you saved the archive to "/mnt/sda1", at the boot prompt enter:

```
knoppix myconfig=/mnt/sda1
```

If it works you will see something like this near the end of the startup messages (Ctrl+Alt+F1):

```
Checking /mnt/sda1 for KNOPPIX configuration file...
Found, now executing /mnt/sda1/knoppix.sh
```

Advanced startup options

"There is only one satisfying way to boot a computer."
— J. H. Goldfuss

Overview

This section explains the bootup options for Knoppix. Use these options to fine-tune Knoppix for your hardware and speed it up.

Enabling DMA

The first and foremost way to make Knoppix version 3.3 run faster that almost every-one can use is to enable DMA. DMA stands for Direct Memory Access. It improves the speed of hard disk drives and it can also help CD-ROM drives. DMA is not supported on all computers, so Knoppix version 3.3 turns it off by default. To enable DMA, add 'dma' to your boot command, for example:

```
knoppix lang=uk dma
```

To test the speed of the hard disk drive, click the Knoppix menu, choose "Root Shell" and enter:

```
hdparm -t /dev/hda
```

Replace "hda" with the device name of your hard drive appropriately. After a pause of about 3 seconds, you will get a little report that will tell you how fast your hard drive reads data. Enabling DMA may make a big difference. For example, look at these sample test results:

Drive	Without DMA	With DMA
Seagate Barracuda 7200 RPM IDE	8.5 MB/sec	26.8 Mb/sec

Note
In Knoppix 3.4 and later, DMA is enabled by default. This means that if you have a more recent version of Knoppix than 3.3, you do not need to set this. To turn off DMA in more recent versions of Knoppix, enter the `nodma` option at the boot prompt.

If you only have a single CD drive

Knoppix takes over your CD drive and you can't eject it during your session. What if you want to use the CD drive for something else? For example, you may want to create CDs using a CD-ReWritable drive. If you only have one CD drive, this will be a problem.

Luckily, there is a solution. It is possible to run Knoppix from a hard drive or RAM, freeing up the CD drive for other tasks.

Transferring to a hard disk partition

Transferring to a hard disk partition means copying the CD contents onto a hard disk. This is called "copying the CD image". Once this is done, Knoppix starts in the normal way but from the hard drive instead the CD-ROM drive.

This gives improved performance, because hard disk drives are generally much faster than CD-ROM drives. It also frees up your CD-ROM drive for other tasks. It does not affect the existing files on the hard drive. All it does is use up hard drive space, which can be reclaimed later.

To transfer to a hard disk partition, you need:

An MS-DOS, FAT or Linux formatted hard disk partition. NTFS (native Windows NT/2000/XP) partitions cannot be used.

At least 700 Mb free space on the partition.

At the boot prompt, enter this command. Replace "device" with the device name of the hard disk partition that you want to use.

```
knoppix tohd=device
```

For example, suppose you have Windows 98. You probably have Windows installed on the first partition of the primary master IDE drive. In this case, use:

```
knoppix tohd=/dev/hda1
```

Knoppix will start from CD, copy itself to the specified device and then continue loading from there. You can then take the Knoppix CD out of the drive.

Re-using an existing image

You only need to copy the CD image to the hard disk once. Next time, you can read back from the hard disk, without having to copy the CD image again.

At the boot prompt, enter this command. Replace "device" with the device name of the hard disk partition where the Knoppix CD image is located.

```
knoppix fromhd=device
```

For example:

```
knoppix fromhd=/dev/hda1
```

Knoppix will start from CD, pick up the CD image from the specified device and continue loading. You can then take the Knoppix CD out of the drive.

Deleting the image

In Windows, remove the "KNOPPIX" directory from the hard drive using Windows Explorer. This will give back the hard drive space occupied by the CD image.

Transferring to RAM

If you have 828 Mb or more of RAM, you can copy the Knoppix CD image to RAM. After an initial wait, transferring to RAM gives dramatically improved performance, and the Knoppix CD is not needed. You need 828 Mb of RAM because the first 700 Mb is used for the CD image. The remaining 128 Mb is used for the system and applications.

At the boot prompt, enter this command:

```
knoppix toram
```

Knoppix will start from CD, transfer the CD image to RAM, and continue loading. Once transfer to RAM has completed, you can take the Knoppix CD out of the drive.

More hardware options

These options let you fine-tune Knoppix for your particular hardware. They can be combined in any order. For example, to start Knoppix with the US language/keyboard, a wheel mouse, a screen resolution of 800x600 and Direct Memory Access (DMA) enabled for hard drives, type this at the boot prompt:

```
knoppix lang=uk wheelmouse screen=800x600 dma
```

Knoppix assumes you have a laptop. It starts up with PCMCIA (credit card adapter) interface support enabled by default. If you have a desktop computer, rather than a laptop, you can improve performance slightly by typing the "nopcmcia" option at the boot prompt. For example, to start the computer with the US locale, a wheel mouse, a screen resolution of 1024x768, and no PCMCIA:

```
knoppix lang=us wheelmouse screen=1024x768 nopcmcia
```

If you have less than 128 Mb RAM

After loading the kernel and the base system, Knoppix looks to see how much RAM is left. The kernel and the base system takes about 20 Mb of RAM. The remainder is called free RAM, or available RAM.

Knoppix checks to see if there is a Linux *swap partition* available. You may have a swap partition if you have previously installed Linux on the hard disk. If so, Knoppix will use the existing swap partition automatically.

If there is less than 80,000 Kb free RAM, Knoppix will prompt you to create a *swap file*. A swap file lets you use part of the hard disk as if it were RAM.

This trick lets you run Knoppix in full, even when you have less than 128 Mb RAM. For example, it is possible to run Knoppix successfully on a computer with only 64 Mb of RAM. However, you pay a performance penalty, because swap is much slower than physical RAM. To create a swap file, you need a hard disk with at least one partition that is formatted with the FAT filesystem. NTFS formatted partitions cannot be used.

1. Start Knoppix in the usual way.

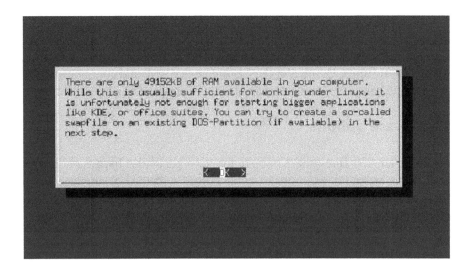

2. You will get a message that says, "There are only X Kb of RAM available in your computer".
3. Press Enter.

4. Knoppix will search for an available FAT formatted partition. If there is more than one, Knoppix will choose the *last* available partition. You will be asked if you want to create a swap file on the partition that Knoppix has selected.

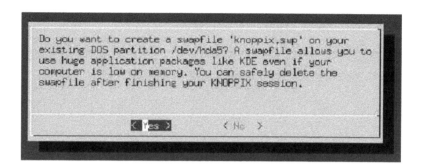

5. Using the arrow keys on the keyboard, choose "Yes", then press Enter.
6. You will be asked how big a swap file you want to create. You need a swap file that is large enough to take the free RAM + swap file total to at least 80,000 Kb.
7. Type the size of the swap file you wish to create. In this example, it says there is 49,152 Kb of physical RAM free. The suggested swap file size of 60 Mb will bring the free total to 108 Mb.

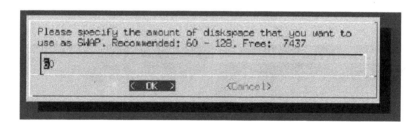

8. Press Enter.
9. Wait for a moment while Knoppix creates the swap file.
10. Press Enter to continue loading Knoppix.

> **Tip**
> Next time you start Knoppix, it will detect and use the swap file automatically. To remove the swap file and reclaim the disk space it occupies, exit Knoppix, start Windows, then delete the file called "knoppix.swp" using Windows Explorer.

Alternatives to KDE

Knoppix has six alternative *desktop managers*. These let you run the X Window System on a computer that doesn't have enough RAM for KDE. They also save loading time, because they load much more quickly.

Ice Window Manager

A small and fast window manager in the Microsoft Windows style.

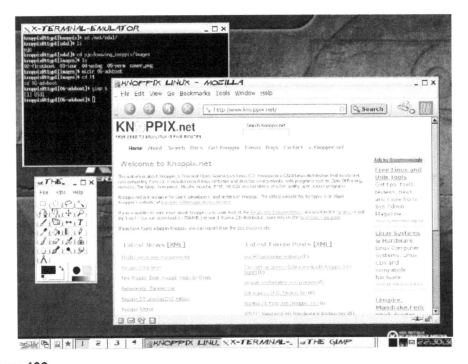

Window Maker

A simple and elegant window manager with a very solid feel.

Fluxbox

Similar in style to Window Maker.

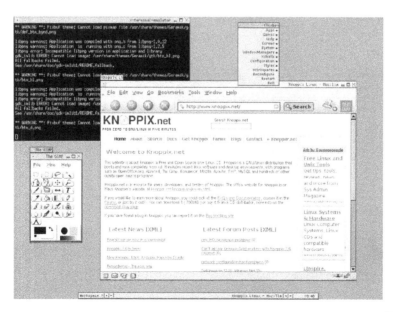

Xfce

Xfce stands for "The Cholesterol Free Desktop Environment".

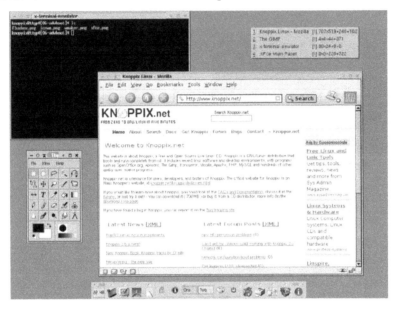

Lars Window Manager

An alternative window manager. In Lars Window Manager, almost everything is done with the keyboard instead of the mouse. Lars Window Manager is designed for programmers that spend most of their time working with text.

Tab Window Manager

TWM is designed to use as little RAM as possible. If you start Knoppix on a compu-ter without enough RAM to run KDE, it will run Tab Window Manager instead.

Starting an alternative window manager

Use one of these commands at the boot prompt.

```
knoppix desktop=icewm       # IceWM
knoppix desktop=wmaker      # Window Maker
knoppix desktop=fluxbox     # Fluxbox
knoppix desktop=xfce        # Xfce
knoppix desktop=larswm      # Lars Window Manager
knoppix desktop=twm         # Tab Window Manager
```

For example, to start Window Maker in the UK locale:

```
knoppix desktop=wmaker lang=uk dma nopcmcia
```

Accessing disks and partitions while outside KDE

You may have noticed there are no desktop disk icons when you are using an alternative to KDE. Luckily, you can still use KDE's disk management tools, even when you are outside KDE. For example:

1. Start Knoppix into Window Maker.
2. Click the "XTerm" icon, which is on the right hand side, second from the top. Enter this command:
   ```
   kdf
   ```

3. Wait while "KDiskFree" starts.
4. Right-click the icon of the disk or partition you want. Click "Mount". Right-click the icon again, then "Open in file manager".

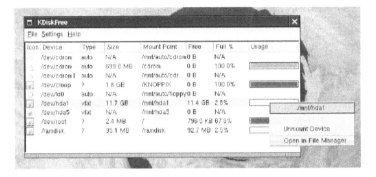

5. The files on the disk or partition will be displayed.

Important: KDiskFree mounts in **read-write** mode, not read-only.

Text mode

Text mode is the fastest way to start Knoppix. Text mode is meant for those who are familiar with the UNIX command line interface. There are many excellent books on the subject, such as "Sams Teach Yourself UNIX in 24 Hours".

Starting

To start Knoppix in text mode, enter this at the boot prompt.

```
knoppix 2
```

For example, to start with UK keyboard/language, with DMA for faster hard disk access, and without PCMCIA because you're not working on a laptop computer, enter:

```
knoppix lang=uk dma nopcmcia 2
```

Leaving

Enter this command to exit Knoppix:

```
halt
```

Localisation

Text mode is called "runlevel 2". When started in text mode, Knoppix uses the "C" locale. The C locale is defined as the "default" locale for applications, meaning that their strings are displayed as written in the initial code, without passing through a translation lookup. Just plain old ASCII. Literally, the "C" locale turns off localisation.

To enable localisation, specify the locale that you want to use with the "lang=" option. For example, enter this at the boot prompt to load Knoppix in text mode with the UK regional settings:

```
knoppix 2 lang=uk
```

Adjusting the keyboard layout

To switch to a UK keyboard layout, type this and press Enter:

```
loadkeys uk
```

The keyboard map will be changed to UK layout.

Accessing disks and partitions

Use the "mount" command. For example, to mount the first partition on the primary master IDE hard drive:

```
cd /mnt
mount hda1
```

The files on the device /dev/hda1 will be mounted to /mnt/hda1. To view the files on the partition:

```
cd hda1
ls
```

The files will be displayed. To learn more about navigating and copying files in text mode, refer to a UNIX manual or text book.

> **Important**
> Disks and partitions are mounted **read-write** by the mount command.

Identifying hardware

Use these commands to get hardware information:

Command	Shows
`lspci`	PCI devices
`lsusb`	USB devices
`cat/proc/cpuinfo`	Processor information
`cat/proc/meminfo`	Random Access Memory details
`cat/proc/scsi/scsi`	SCSI device information
`dmesg`	Kernel messages

Tip

Press Shift + Page Up to see the lines that have scrolled off the top of the screen. Press Shift + Page Down to go back down again.

APPENDICES

Knoppix boot options

knoppix lang=cn|de|da|es|fr|it|nl	specify language/keyboard
knoppix lang=pl|ru|sk|tr|tw|us	specify language/keyboard
knoppix alsa (or alsa=es1938)	Use ALSA sound driver (at your own risk)
knoppix desktop=fluxbox|icewm	Use specified WM instead of KDE (1)
knoppix desktop=kde|larswm|twm	Use specified WM instead of KDE (2)
knoppix desktop=wmaker|xfce	Use specified WM instead of KDE (3)
knoppix screen=1280x1024	Use specified Screen resolution for X
knoppix xvrefresh=60 (or vsync=60)	Use 60 Hz vertical refresh rate for X
knoppix xhrefresh=80 (or hsync=80)	Use 80 kHz horizontal refresh rate for X
knoppix xserver=XFree86|XF86_SVGA	Use specified X-Server
knoppix xmodule=ati|fbdev|i810|mga	Use specified XFree4-Module (1)
knoppix xmodule=nv|radeon|savage|s3	Use specified XFree4-Module (2)
knoppix xmodule=radeon|svga|i810	Use specified XFree4-Module (3)
knoppix 2 Runlevel 2,	Textmode only
knoppix floppyconfig	Run „knoppix.sh" from a floppy
knoppix myconf=/dev/sda1	Run „knoppix.sh" from a partition
knoppix myconf=scan (or config=scan)	Try to find „knoppix.sh" automatically
knoppix home=/dev/sda1/knoppix.img	Mount loopback file as /home/knoppix
knoppix home=scan	Automatic search for knoppix homedir
knoppix no{apic,agp,apm,audio,ddc}	Skip parts of HW-detection (1)
knoppix no{firewire,pcmcia,scsi}	Skip parts of HW-detection (2)
knoppix no{swap,usb}	Skip parts of HW-detection (3)
failsafe	Boot with (almost) no HW-detection
knoppix pci=irqmask=0x0e98	Try this, if PS/2 mouse doesn't work *)
knoppix pci=bios	Workaround for bad PCI controllers
knoppix ide2=0x180 nopcmcia	Boot from PCMCIA-CD-Rom (some notebooks)
knoppix mem=128M	Specify Memory size in MByte
knoppix dma	Enable DMA for ALL IDE-Drives
knoppix noeject	Do NOT eject CD after halt
knoppix noprompt	Do NOT prompt to remove the CD
knoppix vga=normal	No-framebuffer mode, but X
knoppix blind	Start Braille-Terminal (no X)
knoppix brltty=type,port,table	Parameters for Braille device
knoppix wheelmouse	Enable IMPS/2 protocol for wheelmice
knoppix nowheelmouse	Force plain PS/2 protocol for PS/2-mouse
fb1280x1024	Use fixed framebuffer graphics (1)
fb1024x768	Use fixed framebuffer graphics (2)
fb800x600	Use fixed framebuffer graphics (3)
knoppix keyboard=us xkeyboard=us	Use different keyboard (text/X)
knoppix splash	Boot with fancy background splashscreen
knoppix toram	Copy CD to RAM and run from there
knoppix tohd=/dev/hda1	Copy CD to HD partition and run there
knoppix fromhd=/dev/hda1	Boot from previously copied CD-Image
knoppix testcd	Check CD data integrity and md5sums
expert	Interactive setup for experts

GNU General Public Licence

Version 2, June 1991

Copyright (C) 1989, 1991 Free Software Foundation, Inc. 59 Temple Place, Suite 330, Boston, MA 02111-1307 USAEveryone is permitted to copy and distribute verbatim copies of this license document, but changing it is not allowed.

Preamble

The licenses for most software are designed to take away your freedom to share and change it. By contrast, the GNU General Public License is intended to guarantee your freedom to share and change free software—to make sure the software is free for all its users. This General Public License applies to most of the Free Software Foundation's software and to any other program whose authors commit to using it. (Some other Free Software Foundation software is covered by the GNU Library General Public License instead.) You can apply it to your programs, too.

When we speak of free software, we are referring to freedom, not price. Our General Public Licenses are designed to make sure that you have the freedom to distribute copies of free software (and charge for this service if you wish), that you receive source code or can get it if you want it, that you can change the software or use pieces of it in new free programs; and that you know you can do these things.

To protect your rights, we need to make restrictions that forbid anyone to deny you these rights or to ask you to surrender the rights. These restric-tions translate to certain responsibilities for you if you distribute copies of the software, or if you modify it.

For example, if you distribute copies of such a program, whether gratis or for a fee, you must give the recipients all the rights that you have. You must make sure that they, too, receive or can get the source code. And you must show them these terms so they know their rights.

We protect your rights with two steps: (1) copyright the software, and (2) offer you this license which gives you legal permission to copy, distribute and/or modify the software.

Also, for each author's protection and ours, we want to make certain that everyone understands that there is no warranty for this free software. If the software is modified by someone else and passed on, we want its recipients to know that what they have is not the original, so that any problems introduced by others will not reflect on the original authors' reputations.

Finally, any free program is threatened constantly by software patents. We wish to avoid the danger that redistributors of a free program will individua-lly obtain patent licenses, in effect making the program proprietary. To pre-vent this, we have made it clear that any patent must be licensed for every-one's free use or not licensed at all.

The precise terms and conditions for copying, distribution and modification follow.

GNU GENERAL PUBLIC LICENSE
TERMS AND CONDITIONS FOR COPYING, DISTRIBUTION AND MODIFICATION

0. This License applies to any program or other work which contains a notice placed by the copyright holder saying it may be distributed under the terms of this General Public License. The „Program", below, refers to any such program or work, and a „work based on the Program" means either the Program or any

derivative work under copyright law: that is to say, a work containing the Program or a portion of it, either verbatim or with modifications and/or translated into another language. (Hereinafter, translation is included without limitation in the term „modification".) Each licensee is addressed as „you".

Activities other than copying, distribution and modification are not covered by this License; they are outside its scope. The act of running the Program is not restricted, and the output from the Program is covered only if its contents constitute a work based on the Program (independent of having been made by running the Program). Whether that is true depends on what the Program does.

1. You may copy and distribute verbatim copies of the Program's source code as you receive it, in any medium, provided that you conspicuously and appropriately publish on each copy an appropriate copyright notice and disclaimer of warranty; keep intact all the notices that refer to this License and to the absence of any warranty; and give any other recipients of the Program a copy of this License along with the Program.

You may charge a fee for the physical act of transferring a copy, and you may at your option offer warranty protection in exchange for a fee.

2. You may modify your copy or copies of the Program or any portion of it, thus forming a work based on the Program, and copy and distribute such modifications or work under the terms of Section 1 above, provided that you also meet all of these conditions:

a) You must cause the modified files to carry prominent notices stating that you changed the files and the date of any change.

b) You must cause any work that you distribute or publish, that in whole or in part contains or is derived from the Program or any part thereof, to be licensed as a whole at no charge to all third parties under the terms of this   License.

c) If the modified program normally reads commands interactively when run, you must cause it, when started running for such interactive use in the most ordinary way, to print or display an announcement including an appropriate copyright notice and a notice that there is no warranty (or else, saying that you provide a warranty) and that users may redistribute the program under these conditions, and telling the user how to view a copy of this License. (Exception: if the Program itself is interactive but does not normally print such an announcement, your work based on the Program is not required to print an announcement.)

These requirements apply to the modified work as a whole. If identifiable sections of that work are not derived from the Program, and can be reasonably considered independent and separate works in themselves, then this License, and its terms, do not apply to those sections when you distribute them as separate works. But when you distribute the same sections as part of a whole which is a work based on the Program, the distribution of the whole must be on the terms of this License, whose permissions for other licensees extend to the
entire whole, and thus to each and every part regardless of who wrote it.

Thus, it is not the intent of this section to claim rights or contest your rights to work written entirely by you; rather, the intent is to exercise the right to control the distribution of derivative or collective works based on the Program.

In addition, mere aggregation of another work not based on the Program with the Program (or with a work based on the Program) on a volume of a storage or distribution medium does not bring the other work under the scope of this License.

3. You may copy and distribute the Program (or a work based on it, under Section

2) in object code or executable form under the terms of Sections 1 and 2 above provided that you also do one of the following:

a) Accompany it with the complete corresponding machine-readable source code, which must be distributed under the terms of Sections 1 and 2 above on a medium customarily used for software interchange; or,

b) Accompany it with a written offer, valid for at least three years, to give any third party, for a charge no more than your cost of physically performing source distribution, a complete machine-readable copy of the corresponding source code, to be distributed under the terms of Sections 1 and 2 above on a medium customarily used for software interchange; or,

c) Accompany it with the information you received as to the offer to distribute corresponding source code. (This alternative is allowed only for noncommercial distribution and only if you received the program in object code or executable form with such an offer, in accord with Subsection b above.)

The source code for a work means the preferred form of the work for making modifications to it. For an executable work, complete source code means all the source code for all modules it contains, plus any associated interface definition files, plus the scripts used to control compilation and installation of the executable. However, as a special exception, the source code distributed need not include anything that is normally distributed (in either source or binary form) with the major components (compiler, kernel, and so on) of the operating system on which the executable runs, unless that component itself accompanies the executable.

If distribution of executable or object code is made by offering access to copy from a designated place, then offering equivalent access to copy the source code from the same place counts as distribution of the source code, even though third parties are not compelled to copy the source along with the object code.

4. You may not copy, modify, sublicense, or distribute the Program except as expressly provided under this License. Any attempt otherwise to copy, modify, sublicense or distribute the Program is void, and will automatically terminate your rights under this License. However, parties who have received copies, or rights, from you under this License will not have their licenses terminated so long as such parties remain in full compliance.

5. You are not required to accept this License, since you have not signed it. However, nothing else grants you permission to modify or distribute the Program or its derivative works. These actions are prohibited by law if you do not accept this License. Therefore, by modifying or distributing the Program (or any work based on the Program), you indicate your acceptance of this License to do so, and all its terms and conditions for copying, distributing or modifying the Program or works based on it.

6. Each time you redistribute the Program (or any work based on the Program), the recipient automatically receives a license from the original licensor to copy, distribute or modify the Program subject to these terms and conditions. You may not impose any further restrictions on the recipients' exercise of the rights granted herein. You are not responsible for enforcing compliance by third parties to this License.

7. If, as a consequence of a court judgment or allegation of patent infringement or for any other reason (not limited to patent issues), conditions are imposed on you (whether by court order, agreement or otherwise) that contradict the conditions of this License, they do not excuse you from the conditions of this License. If you cannot distribute so as to satisfy simultaneously your obligations under this distribute so as to satisfy simultaneously your obligations under this License and any other pertinent obligations, then as a consequence you may not distribute

the Program at all. For example, if a patent license would not permit royalty-freeredistribution of the Program by all those who receive copies directly or indirectly through you, then the only way you could satisfy both it and this License would be to refrain entirely from distribution of the Program.

If any portion of this section is held invalid or unenforceable under any particular circumstance, the balance of the section is intended to apply and the section as a whole is intended to apply in other circumstances.

It is not the purpose of this section to induce you to infringe any patents or other property right claims or to contest validity of any such claims; this section has the sole purpose of protecting the integrity of the free software distribution system, which is implemented by public license practices. Many people have made generous contributions to the wide range of software distributed through that system in reliance on consistent application of that system; it is up to the author/donor to decide if he or she is willing to distribute software through any other system and a licensee cannot impose that choice.

This section is intended to make thoroughly clear what is believed to be a consequence of the rest of this License.

8. If the distribution and/or use of the Program is restricted in certain countries either by patents or by copyrighted interfaces, the original copyright holder who places the Program under this License may add an explicit geographical distribution limitation excluding those countries, so that distribution is permitted only in or among countries not thus excluded. In such case, this License incorporates the limitation as if written in the body of this License.

9. The Free Software Foundation may publish revised and/or new versions of the General Public License from time to time. Such new versions will be similar in spirit to the present version, but may differ in detail to address new problems or concerns.

Each version is given a distinguishing version number. If the Program specifies a version number of this License which applies to it and „any later version", you have the option of following the terms and conditions either of that version or of any later version published by the Free Software Foundation. If the Program does not specify a version number of this License, you may choose any version ever published by the Free Software Foundation.

10. If you wish to incorporate parts of the Program into other free programs whose distribution conditions are different, write to the author to ask for permission. For software which is copyrighted by the Free Software Foundation, write to the Free Software Foundation; we sometimes make exceptions for this. Our decision will be guided by the two goals of preserving the free status of all derivatives of our free software and of promoting the sharing and reuse of software generally.

NO WARRANTY

11. BECAUSE THE PROGRAM IS LICENSED FREE OF CHARGE, THERE IS NO WARRANTY FOR THE PROGRAM, TO THE EXTENT PERMITTED BY APPLICABLE LAW. EXCEPT WHEN OTHERWISE STATED IN WRITING THE COPYRIGHT HOLDERS AND/OR OTHER PARTIES PROVIDE THE PROGRAM „AS IS" WITHOUT WARRANTY OF ANY KIND, EITHER EXPRESSED OR IMPLIED, INCLUDING, BUT NOT LIMITED TO, THE IMPLIED WARRANTIES OF MERCHANTABILITY AND FITNESS FOR A PARTICULAR PURPOSE. THE ENTIRE RISK AS TO THE QUALITY AND PERFORMANCE OF THE PROGRAM IS WITH YOU. SHOULD THE PROGRAM PROVE DEFECTIVE, YOU ASSUME THE COST OF ALL NECESSARY SERVICING, REPAIR OR CORRECTION.

12. IN NO EVENT UNLESS REQUIRED BY APPLICABLE LAW OR AGREED TO IN WRITING WILL ANY COPYRIGHT HOLDER, OR ANY OTHER PARTY WHO MAY MODIFY AND/OR REDISTRIBUTE THE PROGRAM AS PERMITTED ABOVE, BE LIABLE TO YOU FOR DAMAGES, INCLUDING ANY GENERAL, SPECIAL, INCIDENTAL OR CONSEQUENTIAL DAMAGES ARISING OUT OF THE USE OR INABILITY TO USE THE PROGRAM (INCLUDING BUT NOT LIMITED TO LOSS OF DATA OR DATA BEING RENDERED INACCURATE OR LOSSES SUSTAINED BY YOU OR THIRD PARTIES OR A FAILURE OF THE PROGRAM TO OPERATE WITH ANY OTHER PROGRAMS), EVEN IF SUCH HOLDER OR OTHER PARTY HAS BEEN ADVISED OF THE POSSIBILITY OF SUCH DAMAGES.

END OF TERMS AND CONDITIONS

GNU Free Documentation License Version 1.2, November 2002 Copyright (C)

2000,2001,2002 Free Software Foundation, Inc. 51 Franklin St, Fifth Floor, Boston, MA 02110-1301 USA Everyone is permitted to copy and distribute verbatim copies of this license document, but changing it is not allowed.

0. PREAMBLE

The purpose of this License is to make a manual, textbook, or other functional and useful document „free" in the sense of freedom: to assure everyone the effective freedom to copy and redistribute it, with or without modifying it, either commercially or noncommercially. Secondarily, this License preserves for the author and publisher a way to get credit for their work, while not being considered responsible for modifications made by others.

This License is a kind of „copyleft", which means that derivative works of the document must themselves be free in the same sense. It complements the GNU General Public License, which is a copyleft license designed for free software.

We have designed this License in order to use it for manuals for free software, because free software needs free documentation: a free program should come with manuals providing the same freedoms that the software does. But this License is not limited to software manuals; it can be used for any textual work, regardless of subject matter or whether it is published as a printed book. We recommend this License principally for works whose purpose is instruction or reference.

1. APPLICABILITY AND DEFINITIONS

This License applies to any manual or other work, in any medium, that contains a notice placed by the copyright holder saying it can be distributed under the terms of this License. Such a notice grants a world-wide, royalty-free license, unlimited in duration, to use that work under the conditions stated herein. The „Document", below, refers to any such manual or work. Any member of the public is a licensee, and is addressed as „you". You accept the license if you copy, modify or distribute the work in a way requiring permission under copyright law.

A „Modified Version" of the Document means any work containing the Document or a portion of it, either copied verbatim, or with modifications and/or translated into another language.

A „Secondary Section" is a named appendix or a front-matter section of the Document that deals exclusively with the relationship of the publishers or authors of the Document to the Document's overall subject (or to related matters) and contains nothing that could fall directly within that overall subject. (Thus, if the Document is in part a textbook of mathematics, a Secondary Section may not explain any mathematics.) The relationship could be a matter of historical connection with the subject or with related matters, or of legal, commercial, philosophical, ethical or political position regarding them.

The „Invariant Sections" are certain Secondary Sections whose titles are designated, as being those of Invariant Sections, in the notice that says that the Document is released under this License. If a section does not fit the above definition of Secondary then it is not allowed to be designated as Invariant. The Document may contain zero Invariant Sections. If the Document does not identify any Invariant Sections then there are none.

The „Cover Texts" are certain short passages of text that are listed, as Front-Cover Texts or Back-Cover Texts, in the notice that says that the Document is released under this License. A Front-Cover Text may be at most 5 words, and a

Back-Cover Text may be at most 25 words.

A „Transparent" copy of the Document means a machine-readable copy, represented in a format whose specification is available to the general public, that is suitable for revising the document straightforwardly with generic text editors or (for images composed of pixels) generic paint programs or (for drawings) some widely available drawing editor, and that is suitable for input to text formatters or for automatic translation to a variety of formats suitable for input to text formatters. A copy made in an otherwise Transparent file format whose markup, or absence of markup, has been arranged to thwart or discourage subsequent modification by readers is not Transparent. An image format is not Transparent if used for any substantial amount of text. A copy that is not „Transparent" is called „Opaque".

Examples of suitable formats for Transparent copies include plain ASCII without markup, Texinfo input format, LaTeX input format, SGML or XML using a publicly available DTD, and standard-conforming simple HTML, PostScript or PDF designed for human modification. Examples of transparent image formats include PNG, XCF and JPG. Opaque formats include proprietary formats that can be read and edited only by proprietary word processors, SGML or XML for which the DTD and/or processing tools are not generally available, and the machine-generated HTML, PostScript or PDF produced by some word processors for output purposes only.

The „Title Page" means, for a printed book, the title page itself, plus such following pages as are needed to hold, legibly, the material this License requires to appear in the title page. For works in formats which do not have any title page as such, „Title Page" means the text near the most prominent appearance of the work's title, preceding the beginning of the body of the text.

A section „Entitled XYZ" means a named subunit of the Document whose title either is precisely XYZ or contains XYZ in parentheses following text that translates XYZ in another language. (Here XYZ stands for a specific section name mentioned below, such as „Acknowledgements", „Dedications", „Endorsements", or „History".) To „Preserve the Title" of such a section when you modify the Document means that it remains a section „Entitled XYZ" according to this definition.

The Document may include Warranty Disclaimers next to the notice which states that this License applies to the Document. These Warranty Disclaimers are considered to be included by reference in this License, but only as regards disclaiming warranties: any other implication that these Warranty Disclaimers may have is void and has no effect on the meaning of this License.

2. VERBATIM COPYING

You may copy and distribute the Document in any medium, either commercially or noncommercially, provided that this License, the copyright notices, and the license notice saying this License applies to the Document are reproduced in all copies, and that you add no other conditions whatsoever to those of this License. You may not use technical measures to obstruct or control the reading or further copying of the copies you make or distribute. However, you may accept compensation in exchange for copies. If you distribute a large enough number of copies you must also follow the conditions in section 3.

You may also lend copies, under the same conditions stated above, and you may publicly display copies.

3. COPYING IN QUANTITY

If you publish printed copies (or copies in media that commonly have printed covers) of the Document, numbering more than 100, and the Document's license notice requires Cover Texts, you must enclose the copies in covers that carry, clearly and legibly, all these Cover Texts: Front-Cover Texts on the front cover, and Back-Cover Texts on the back cover. Both covers must also clearly and legibly identify you as the publisher of these copies. The front cover must present the full title with all words of the title equally prominent and visible. You may add other material on the covers in addition. Copying with changes limited to the covers, as long as they preserve the title of the Document and satisfy these conditions, can be treated as verbatim copying in other respects.

If the required texts for either cover are too voluminous to fit legibly, you should put the first ones listed (as many as fit reasonably) on the actual cover, and continue the rest onto adjacent pages.

If you publish or distribute Opaque copies of the Document numbering more than 100, you must either include a machine-readable Transparent copy along with each Opaque copy, or state in or with each Opaque copy a computer-network location from which the general network-using public has access to download using public-standard network protocols a complete Transparent copy of the Document, free of added material. If you use the latter option, you must take reasonably prudent steps, when you begin distribution of Opaque copies in quantity, to ensure that this Transparent copy will remain thus accessible at the stated location until at least one year after the last time you distribute an Opaque copy (directly or through your agents or retailers) of that edition to the public.

It is requested, but not required, that you contact the authors of the Document well before redistributing any large number of copies, to give them a chance to provide you with an updated version of the Document.

4. MODIFICATIONS

You may copy and distribute a Modified Version of the Document under the conditions of sections 2 and 3 above, provided that you release the Modified Version under precisely this License, with the Modified Version filling the role of the Document, thus licensing distribution and modification of the Modified Version to whoever possesses a copy of it. In addition, you must do these things in the Modified Version:

A. Use in the Title Page (and on the covers, if any) a title distinct from that of the Document, and from those of previous versions (which should, if there were any, be listed in the History section of the Document). You may use the same title as a previous version if the original publisher of that version gives permission.
B. List on the Title Page, as authors, one or more persons or entities responsible for authorship of the modifications in the Modified Version, together with at least five of the principal authors of the Document (all of its principal authors, if it has fewer than five), unless they release you from this requirement.
C. State on the Title page the name of the publisher of the Modified Version, as the publisher.
D. Preserve all the copyright notices of the Document.
E. Add an appropriate copyright notice for your modifications adjacent to the other copyright notices.
F. Include, immediately after the copyright notices, a license notice giving the public permission to use the Modified Version under the terms of this License, in the form shown in the Addendum below.
G. Preserve in that license notice the full lists of Invariant Sections and required Cover Texts given in the Document's license notice.
H. Include an unaltered copy of this License.
I. Preserve the section Entitled „History", Preserve its Title, and add to it an item stating at least the title, year, new authors, and publisher of the Modified Version as given on the Title Page. If there is no section Entitled „History" in the Document, create one stating the title, year, authors, and publisher of the Document as given on its Title Page, then add an item describing the Modified Version as stated in the previous sentence.
J. Preserve the network location, if any, given in the Document for public access to a Transparent copy of the Document, and likewise the network locations

given in the Document for previous versions it was based on. These may be placed in the „History" section. You may omit a network location for a work that was published at least four years before the Document itself, or if the original publisher of the version it refers to gives permission.

K. For any section Entitled „Acknowledgements" or „Dedications", Preserve the Title of the section, and preserve in the section all the substance and tone of each of the contributor acknowledgements and/or dedications given therein.

L. Preserve all the Invariant Sections of the Document, unaltered in their text and in their titles. Section numbers or the equivalent are not considered part of the section titles.

M. Delete any section Entitled „Endorsements". Such a section may not be included in the Modified Version.

N. Do not retitle any existing section to be Entitled „Endorsements" or to conflict in title with any Invariant Section.

O. Preserve any Warranty Disclaimers.

If the Modified Version includes new front-matter sections or appendices that qualify as Secondary Sections and contain no material copied from the Document, you may at your option designate some or all of these sections as invariant. To do this, add their titles to the list of Invariant Sections in the Modified Version's license notice. These titles must be distinct from any other section titles.

You may add a section Entitled „Endorsements", provided it contains nothing but endorsements of your Modified Version by various parties—for example, statements of peer review or that the text has been approved by an organization as the authoritative definition of a standard.

You may add a passage of up to five words as a Front-Cover Text, and a passage of up to 25 words as a Back-Cover Text, to the end of the list of Cover Texts in the Modified Version. Only one passage of Front-Cover Text and one of Back-Cover Text may be added by (or through arrangements made by) any one entity. If the Document already includes a cover text for the same cover, previously added by you or by arrangement made by the same entity you are acting on behalf of, you may not add another; but you may replace the old one, on explicit permission from the previous publisher that added the old one.

The author(s) and publisher(s) of the Document do not by this License give permission to use their names for publicity for or to assert or imply endorsement of any Modified Version.

5. COMBINING DOCUMENTS

You may combine the Document with other documents released under this License, under the terms defined in section 4 above for modified versions, provided that you include in the combination all of the Invariant Sections of all of the original documents, unmodified, and list them all as Invariant Sections of your combined work in its license notice, and that you preserve all their Warranty Disclaimers.

The combined work need only contain one copy of this License, and multiple identical Invariant Sections may be replaced with a single copy. If there are multiple Invariant Sections with the same name but different contents, make the title of each such section unique by adding at the end of it, in parentheses, the name of the original author or publisher of that section if known, or else a unique number. Make the same adjustment to the section titles in the list of Invariant Sections in the license notice of the combined work.

In the combination, you must combine any sections Entitled „History" in the various original documents, forming one section Entitled „History"; likewise combine any sections Entitled „Acknowledgements", and any sections Entitled „Dedications". You must delete all sections Entitled „Endorsements".

6. COLLECTIONS OF DOCUMENTS

You may make a collection consisting of the Document and other documents released under this License, and replace the individual copies of this License in the various documents with a single copy that is included in the collection, provided that you follow the rules of this License for verbatim copying of each of the documents in all other respects.

You may extract a single document from such a collection, and distribute it individually under this License, provided you insert a copy of this License into the extracted document, and follow this License in all other respects regarding verbatim copying of that document.

7. AGGREGATION WITH INDEPENDENT WORKS

A compilation of the Document or its derivatives with other separate and independent documents or works, in or on a volume of a storage or distribution medium, is called an „aggregate" if the copyright resulting from the compilation is not used to limit the legal rights of the compilation's users beyond what the individual works permit. When the Document is included in an aggregate, this License does not apply to the other works in the aggregate which are not themselves derivative works of the Document.

If the Cover Text requirement of section 3 is applicable to these copies of the Document, then if the Document is less than one half of the entire aggregate, the Document's Cover Texts may be placed on covers that bracket the Document within the aggregate, or the electronic equivalent of covers if the Document is in electronic form. Otherwise they must appear on printed covers that bracket the whole aggregate.

8. TRANSLATION

Translation is considered a kind of modification, so you may distribute translations of the Document under the terms of section 4. Replacing Invariant Sections with translations requires special permission from their copyright holders, but you may include translations of some or all Invariant Sections in addition to the original versions of these Invariant Sections. You may include a translation of this License, and all the license notices in the Document, and any Warranty Disclaimers, provided that you also include the original English version of this License and the original versions of those notices and disclaimers. In case of a disagreement between the translation and the original version of this License or a notice or disclaimer, the original version will prevail.

If a section in the Document is Entitled „Acknowledgements", „Dedications", or „History", the requirement (section 4) to Preserve its Title (section 1) will typically require changing the actual title.

9. TERMINATION You may not copy, modify, sublicense, or distribute the Document except as expressly provided for under this License. Any other attempt to copy, modify, sublicense or distribute the Document is void, and will automatically terminate your rights under this License. However, parties who have received copies, or rights, from you under this License will not have their licenses terminated so long as such parties remain in full compliance.

10. FUTURE REVISIONS OF THIS LICENSE

The Free Software Foundation may publish new, revised versions of the GNU Free Documentation License from time to time. Such new versions will be similar in spirit to the present version, but may differ in detail to address new problems or concerns. See http://www.gnu.org/copyleft/. Each version of the License is given a distinguishing version number. If the Document specifies that a particular numbered version of this License „or any later version" applies to it, you have the option of following the terms and conditions either of that specified version or of any later version that has been published (not as a draft) by the Free Software Foundation. If the Document does not specify a version number of this License, you may choose any version ever published (not as a draft) by the Free Software Foundation.

Index

Index

Index

ONE HUNDRED electronic circuits with
ready to use pcb design layouts!

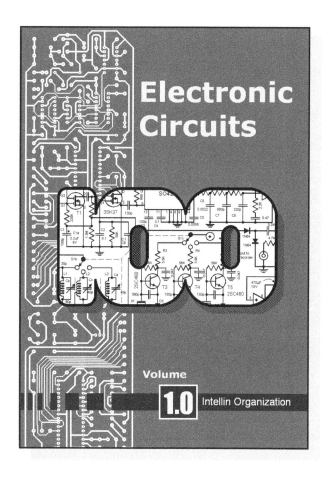

Get your copy now from
amazon.com!

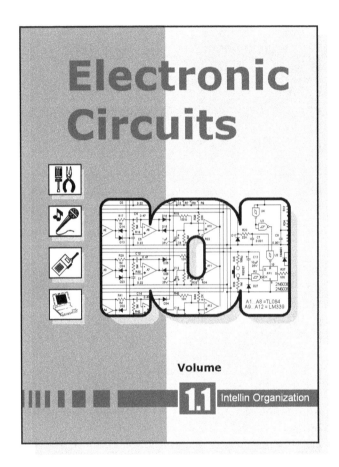

ONE HUNDRED and TWO circuits with
ready to use pcb design layouts!

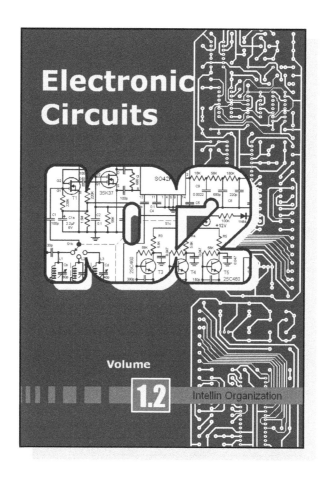

ONE HUNDRED and THREE circuits with
ready to use pcb design layouts!

Get your copy now from
amazon.com!

This authoritative and well-researched book is the only one available that will give you all of the most important and reliable on VHF antenna construction techniques.

This unique book offers a superb collection of detailed, easy-to-follow, fully illustrated, and tested designs, covering such types of antennas as:

Omnidirectional antennas

Gain-omni antennas

Gain-directed beams

Portable antennas

Yagi antennas

Stacked arrays

Stacked collinears

Wideband-omni antennas

THIRD EDITION

PRACTICAL ANTENNA DESIGN

140-150 MHz VHF Transceivers

ELPIDIO LATORILLA

Get your copy now from amazon.com!

A compilation of audio circuits with
ready to use pcb design layouts!

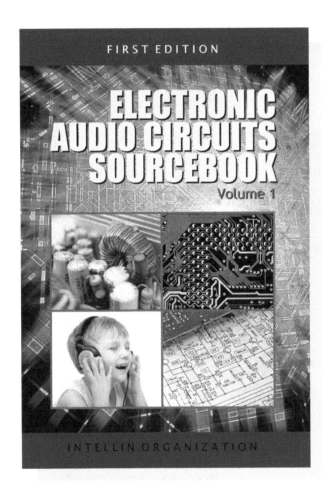

Get your copy now from
amazon.com!

A compilation of power supply circuits with ready to use pcb design layouts!

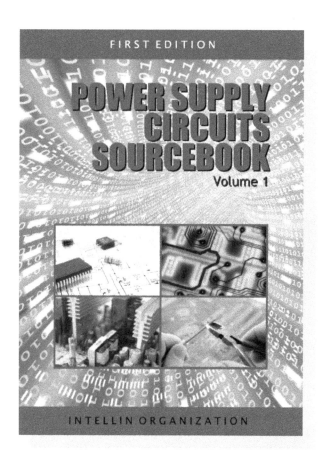

Get your copy now from amazon.com!

www.ingramcontent.com/pod-product-compliance
Lightning Source LLC
Chambersburg PA
CBHW080426060326
40689CB00019B/4395